Skill Development in Counselor Education

Skill Development in Counselor Education provides counselor educators in training with a variety of materials and suggestions to assist in building fundamental skills. Templates, activities, and quizzes guide educators in developing their identities and teaching philosophies, developing engaging curricula, teaching cultural and technological competence, and dealing with complex ethical issues in the classroom. The book also covers a variety of practical topics related to seeking a faculty position or navigating an academic appointment, including writing a CV and cover letter, preparing for interviews, and navigating the tenure process.

Joy S. Whitman, PhD, is a core faculty member of Counseling@Northwestern at the Family Institute at Northwestern University and has over two decades of experience as a counselor and counselor educator.

Laura R. Haddock, PhD, is full-time clinical faculty at Southern New Hampshire University and has more than two decades of experience as a clinician and a counselor educator.

Skill Development in Counselor Education

A Comprehensive Workbook

Edited by
Joy S. Whitman and
Laura R. Haddock

Routledge
Taylor & Francis Group

NEW YORK AND LONDON

First published 2019
by Routledge
711 Third Avenue, New York, NY 10017

and by Routledge
2 Park Square, Milton Park, Abingdon, Oxon, OX14 4RN

Routledge is an imprint of the Taylor & Francis Group, an informa business

Library of Congress Cataloging-in-Publication Data
Names: Whitman, Joy S., editor. | Haddock, Laura R., editor.
Title: Skill development in counselor education: a comprehensive workbook /
edited by Joy S. Whitman and Laura R. Haddock.
Description: New York : Routledge, 2018. | Includes bibliographical
references and index.
Identifiers: LCCN 2018013265 (print) | LCCN 2018030902 (ebook) |
ISBN 9781315413938 (eBook) | ISBN 9781138695542 (hardback) |
ISBN 9781138695559 (pbk.) | ISBN 9781315413938 (ebk)
Subjects: LCSH: Counselors—Study and teaching. | Counselors—Training of.
Classification: LCC BF636.65 (ebook) | LCC BF636.65 .S55 2018 (print) |
DDC 158.3071—dc23
LC record available at https://lccn.loc.gov/2018013265

ISBN: 978-1-138-69554-2 (hbk)
ISBN: 978-1-138-69555-9 (pbk)
ISBN: 978-1-315-41393-8 (ebk)

Typeset in Helvetica
by Florence Production Ltd, Stoodleigh, Devon, UK

Contents

How to Search for Faculty Positions   151
Joy S. Whitman

How to Prepare for an Interview (Sample Questions)   152
Joy S. Whitman

Strategies When Seeking Promotion and Tenure   153
Joy S. Whitman

List of Contributors

Eric T. Beeson, PhD, is a Core Faculty member with The Family Institute at Northwestern University and serves as an Associate Editor of the Journal of Mental Health Counseling. Eric is a long-time advocate for digital learning and bolsters a diverse research agenda focusing on sense of community in higher education, neuroscience in counseling, and ally training programs in higher education.

Esther Benoit received her MEd in marriage couples and family counseling and PhD in Counselor Education from the College of William and Mary. As a licensed professional counselor in the state of Virginia, she continues to work with at-risk youth and their parents in both group and family counseling settings. She is currently faculty in the Clinical Mental Health program at Southern New Hampshire University. Her research interests include moral development, military families, and counselor education and supervision.

Kristi Cannon received an MA in Community Counseling and a PhD in Counselor Education & Supervision from St. Mary's University. She is a licensed professional counselor, nationally certified counselor, and serves as Clinical Faculty for Southern New Hampshire University. Dr. Cannon regularly presents research at the state and national levels and publishes scholarly writings for professional counseling journals and textbooks. Her research interests include counselor development, Relational-Cultural Theory, and assessment practices in higher education.

J. Kelly Coker, PhD, is an Associate Professor in the Department of Counseling at Palo Alto University. She has been a professional counselor since 1992 and a counselor educator in CACREP accredited programs since

1998. Dr. Coker is a licensed professional counselor in North Carolina, and she has worked in school, private practice, and tele-behavioral health settings with children, adolescents, adults, and couples. Dr. Coker has multiple professional publications and presentations, and she currently serves as the Chair of the CACREP Board.

Abby E. Dougherty, PhD, is an Assistant Professor at Drexel University in the Creative Art Therapies and Counseling program. She received her master's in Mental Health Counseling, and her doctorate in Counselor Education and Supervision, both through Walden University. Abby is the President for the Greater Philadelphia Pennsylvania Counseling Association. Her interests include examining the experience of students with learning disabilities in higher education, relational-cultural theory, and using mindfulness and contemplative tools in counselor education.

Stephanie Fellenger is an Ohio-Licensed Professional Clinical Counselor with Supervisory Endorsement. Ms. Fellenger earned an MSEd in Clinical Mental Health and Addictions Counseling as well as an MA in English from Youngstown State University, a BA in liberal arts from The Ohio State University, and is currently a doctoral student in the Counselor Education and Supervision program at Walden University. Ms. Fellenger has experience in a variety of clinical settings and currently works in private practice.

Laura R. Haddock, PhD, LPC-S, NCC, ACS currently serves as a full-time member of the Clinical Faculty for the Clinical Mental Health Program at Southern New Hampshire University. Dr. Haddock routinely presents and publishes scholarly works and was the recipient of the 2017 Association of Counselor Education and Supervision Distinguished Service Award—Counselor Educator. Her research interests include counselor wellness and secondary trauma, graduate student development and remediation, cultural diversity, and supervision.

Marcella Rolle is currently enrolled as a doctoral student at Walden University pursuing a degree in Counselor Education and Supervision. Professionally, Marcella provides small group enrichment, academic, and wellness services to middle school students and their families through an afterschool program in Southwest Georgia. In her free time Marcella offers training to encourage cultural competence and awareness in Southwest Georgia.

Dr. Sheila N. Russell is a licensed professional counselor in Texas and a nationally certified counselor through the National Board of Certified Counselors. She received her doctorate in Counselor Education and Supervision in 2017. Dr. Russell specializes in child, adolescent, and family counseling. She is committed to conducting research focused on best clinical services and practices to these populations through counselor education and supervision.

Dr. Ljubica Spiro has been a counselor educator for over 12 years. She has taught counseling courses in the USA and abroad. She is a licensed professional clinical counselor in the state of Ohio, a licensed professional counselor and a certified professional clinical supervisor in the state of Georgia. Her research interests include multicultural issues in counseling and supervision, international counseling, and cross-cultural mentoring. Her clinical experience includes treating adolescents, adults, couples and families, specializing in the treatment of severe and persistent mental health issues.

Jenae Thompson, MEd, LPC, NCC, is a Doctoral Candidate studying Counselor Education and Supervision and is the owner of Synergy Counseling Services, LLC. She is passionate about systematically addressing issues of marginalization many clients experience especially those relative to racial and ethnic minorities, children, the LGBT community, and women. Her research interests include counselor educator cognitive development, clinical applications of the multicultural and social justice competencies, intersectionality pedagogy, and culturally sensitive gatekeeping.

Joy S. Whitman, PhD, is Core Faculty in the Counseling@Northwestern master's program at The Family Institute at Northwestern University. Prior to this position, she was Core Faculty at Walden University, Associate Professor at DePaul University, and Associate Professor at Purdue University Calumet. Her research focus is on LGBTQ counseling issues, specifically on training counselors to provide affirmative therapeutic treatment. Joy is a Licensed Clinical Professional Counselor in Illinois and a Licensed Professional Counselor in Missouri.

Preface

This supplemental workbook is intended to be used in concert with *Preparing the Educator in Counselor Education: A Comprehensive Guide to Building Knowledge and Developing Skills*, and yet it can stand alone as its own activity workbook or be used in conjunction with other resources. It is our hope that this collection of examples and experiential activities will help facilitate conceptual understanding and applied understanding. The activities are organized around the themes of the chapter of the text and are focused on using the information from the text in practical and useful ways. For example, in chapter 7 we offer you a sample syllabus to help you create your own, and in chapter 6 we offer an exercise for creating learning objectives. Chapter 12 is the only chapter that is not also included in the text, and in this chapter we wanted to help you prepare for a career in academia through activities such as creating a cv and planning for an interview. We hope you find the workbook valuable for helping you strengthen your professional identity into a counselor educator who is ethical, professional, and ready for a career in academia.

Joy S. Whitman and Laura R. Haddock

Acknowledgments

I want to thank Danica Rodriguez for your assistance in organizing the material for this workbook. Your attention to the details and your enthusiasm in doing made the process seamless. I also want to thank the contributors of this workbook whose creativity and experience brought these activities to life. Finally, I want to thank the students I've known through the years whose desire to become ethical counselors and counselor educators taught me how to be a counselor educator. You will never know how much your trust in me and our work together means to me.

Joy S. Whitman

I want to thank all of my friends, colleagues, and students who contributed to this work. Your demonstration of such an electric spirit of professional service reminded me, yet again, what a privilege it is to be part of such a supportive network. Your talent is truly inspiring! It has been a delightful experience to watch those who are growing, those who are teaching, and those who are masters all come together to create a tool to give back to those that want to be learn! You honor me with your generosity and I thank you!

Laura R. Haddock

1 Establishing an Identity as a Counselor Educator

The supplemental materials in this chapter are included to assist building insight into the professional identity characteristics that produce, promote, and foster learning, and explore what qualities make for effective and influential teachers. They will include:

- Experiential exercises for self-awareness and to strengthen teaching

- Guided activity to explore personal characteristics that may foster and hinder effective teaching

- Questions to deepen your self-reflection about your identity as an educator in counselor education

- Quiz

Experiential Exercises for Self-Awareness and to Strengthen Teaching

Laura R. Haddock

In order to promote a connection between self-reflection and your teaching, begin by determining what you want to focus on. It may be that you would like to emphasize a particular element of your teaching process or examine student connection, or how to strengthen the delivery of course content. Whatever you choose, begin by collecting information.

Here are a few ways that you can do this:

Keep a Journal

A journal is an easy way to reflect upon what happens during your instruction. With consideration for the area you want to focus on, jot down a few notes describing your reactions and feelings to your own work and then, if helpful, follow up with any observations you have about your students.

Video Recording

A video recording of your teaching is valuable because it provides an unaltered and unbiased vantage point for how effective your lesson may be from both a teacher and student perspective. Record yourself teaching, watch the recording, and reflect on your observations.

Student Observation

Student feedback is frequently offered to faculty members at the end of each term. Think critically about the feedback. Take note of your reactions and reflect on what this information might mean to your teaching process.

Peer Observation

Invite a colleague to observe your teaching. Give your peer questions that you would like to have the answers to regarding your teaching such as whether the students seemed to be engaged or understand the material. Take some time to collaborate after the observation and hear your colleagues feedback and answers to your questions. Reflect on the information.

Analyze and Implement Effective Techniques

Now that you have collected the information, it's time to analyze it. The first thing you should look for is any recurring patterns. If you video recorded your lesson, did you find anything that kept happening over and over? Look at your student feedback. Did any themes emerge?

Self-Reflection on Desirable Clinical and Teaching Skills

The ultimate goal of self-reflection is to strengthen the way you teach. Self-reflection is a technique that can help you increase your self-concept and maximize your potential as an instructor. Explore your skills by engaging in the following activity.

Take a piece of paper and label one side "Counselor" and the other side "Teacher". Starting with counselor, make a list of skills that you feel serve you best in your clinical work. Make the list reflective of both interpersonal dynamics and clinical skill. For example, you might include characteristics like genuine, large vocabulary of feeling words, and knowledgeable about multiple counseling techniques and interventions. on your list of descriptions for a good counselor. Next, flip to the other side and using your own life experience and your current impressions, make a list of the interpersonal dynamics and teaching skills that you feel are necessary to be successful as a teacher. For example, you might include, competent in counseling theory and human growth and development, knowledgeable about learning theory, talented in generating individualized feedback. After you have completed both lists, consider which items seem to naturally transfer and/or are included on both lists. Next consider what skills you have identified as important for teaching that you still need to learn.

Guided Activity to Explore Personal Characteristics That May Foster and Hinder Effective Teaching

Sheila N. Russell

Think about a past teacher that you admired or favored. Create a visual concept map that identifies your personal characteristics. Then color in the bubbles yellow that you think are characteristics that foster effective teaching, and color in the bubbles red that you think hinder effective teaching. Make sure you consider things that inspire and motivate you, as well as personal biases that might hinder effective teaching. An example of a concept map is provided below.

Figure 1.1

Questions to Deepen Your Self-Reflection About Your Identity as an Educator in Counselor Education

Jenae Thompson and Joy S. Whitman

- What personal and professional experiences led you to becoming a counselor educator?
- How have these experienced shaped the way you teach or plan to teach counselors-in-training (CIT)? Provide examples.
- What personal characteristics, traits, and skills do you believe you have that will contribute to your identity as an educator? What will detract? What do you plan to do to enhance those characteristics, traits, and skills that will contribute and reduce those that will detract?
- How does your identity as a counselor influence your identity as an educator? What skills and knowledge as a counselor do you imagine transferring to your skill and knowledge base as a counselor educator?
- Beyond the knowledge and skills that students learn in counseling programs, what do you hope future counseling students gain from their

experience with you as their educator? What professional characteristics as a counselor do you expect will influence your identity as a counselor educator and impact the experience students have with you?

Quiz

1. Which of the following is not considered part of the teaching role?

   a. Classroom instruction
   b. Supervision of practicum/internship students
   c. Publishing or presenting original research
   d. Mentoring doctoral students

2. Critical Thinking and problem solving are one of three critical components of:

   a. Teaching
   b. Service
   c. Scholarship
   d. None of the above

3. According to the Carnegie Classifications of Institutions of Higher Learning, Research I schools give high priority to:

   a. Research
   b. Teaching
   c. Service
   d. Teacher wellness

4. Counselor Educators are mandated to be skilled as clinicians and teachers by which of the following?

   a. University Employment Contracts
   b. ACA Code of Ethics
   c. Doctoral degree requirements
   d. Counselor Educator Oath of Responsibility

5. Who said the following: "If you can't explain it simply, you don't understand it well enough"?

   a. Frank Parsons
   b. Sam Gladding
   c. Albert Einstein
   d. Donald Trump

6. Which of the following are not mentioned as a reason that adults routinely return to graduate school?

   a. Professional image
   b. Higher wages
   c. Increased career opportunities
   d. Both A and C

7. Strong relational connections with students may result in:

   a. Increased interest in the teacher's professional experiences
   b. More cooperative students
   c. Better attendance
   d. Having students submit work on time

8. Faculty members may expect to participate in professional service throughout their career in the areas of:

   a. University Service
   b. Service to the Profession
   c. Service to the Community
   d. One or all of these

9. Counselor Educators are commonly expected to participate in which of the following activities as part of a faculty role?

   a. Teaching
   b. Service
   c. Scholarship
   d. All of the above

10. Effective teaching requires a willingness to cast a critical eye on the process and your own role in that process.

   a. True
   b. False

11. Learning to be an instructor for adult learners requires a dedication to understanding your students and taking responsibility for growing the skills and professional dispositions that contribute to teaching excellence.

   a. True
   b. False

12. Experienced counselor educators tend to become increasingly less active in service over the course of their careers.

    a. True
    b. False

13. CACREP (2016) maintains guidelines that require a strict faculty student ratio that full time students should not exceed full time faculty by more than 20:1.

    a. True
    b. False

14. A primary component of scholarship is production, conceptualization, and understanding of new knowledge.

    a. True
    b. False

15. The roles of teaching, scholarship and service are static and tasks beyond that of instructor do not have teaching components.

    a. True
    b. False

2 Developing a Personal Philosophy of Teaching

The activities in this chapter are designed to assist with the development of personal teaching philosophy. Integral to the creation of a teaching philosophy is knowledge of theories of learning and teaching. The supplemental material will include:

- Mapping template of learning theories and teaching with your personal characteristics and beliefs

- Template for personal philosophy of teaching statement

- Philosophy of teaching statement examples

- Teaching philosophy self-reflection

- Quiz

Mapping Template of Learning Theories and Teaching with Your Personal Characteristics and Beliefs

Sheila N. Russell

Create a visual map of a modern theory of learning and teaching. Then add to the map your own personal characteristics and beliefs about each theory. An example of a concept map is provided below in Figure 2.1.

Template for Personal Philosophy of Teaching Statement

Joy S. Whitman

Learning Goals

- What do you want students to learn about counseling?
- How is the acquisition of knowledge, skills, and dispositions connected to learning counseling as a practice?
- If a student were to recommend your class to another student, what would you want the student to say in regard to what they learned in your classes?
- How are specific issues of ethics, diversity, and advocacy weaved through student learning?

Teaching Methods and Enactment of Goals

- What are the roles and responsibilities of students and teachers in the process of learning?
- What theories of learning and counseling inform your beliefs about how students learn and the methods you use to teach?
- How do your methods help adult learners reach your goals of learning?
- How do your personal characteristics and values relate to your choice and implementation of your teaching methods?
- How do the methods vary along on-line and face-to-face platforms and how are they similar?

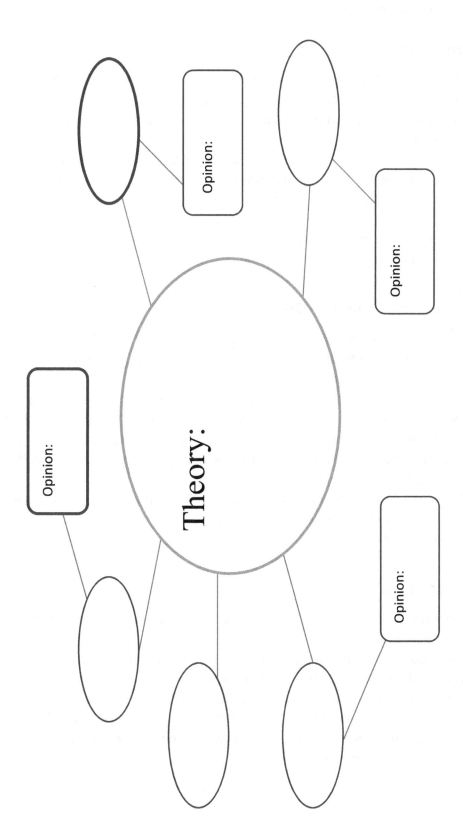

Figure 2.1 Mapping Template

Learning Environment

- What kind of learning environment do I want to create for adult learners?
- How does the creation of this learning environment connect to my beliefs and values and to my theoretical orientation and convictions about learning and teaching?
- How do I create an inclusive environment that addresses the various styles of student learning and diversity of student identities? How do I create this both in on-line and face-to-face platforms?
- What is my approach to managing the learning environment so that all students feel included while modeling the values of the counseling profession?

Assessment of Learning Goals

- How do I know students are learning?
- What assessments of student learning do I use that are consistent with my understanding of learning and counseling?
- How are the goals of learning assessed formatively and summatively?
- How do students know they are learning? What have I developed to help them self-assess their own progress toward learning goals? How are those processes integrated with my philosophy of learning and theoretical orientation of counseling?
- How do I understand and enact my roles as gatekeeper in the counseling profession via assessment of student learning and dispositional development?

Assessment of Teaching

- How do I know my teaching methods are effective and assess what I intend to assess?
- How do I use teaching evaluations to strengthen and transform my approach and philosophy of student learning?
- What are my strengths as a teacher, and how are those strengths connected to my identity as a counselor and counselor educator?
- How do I enact my role as reflective practitioner to improve my teaching and continue to develop?

Philosophy of Teaching Statement Examples

Stephanie Fellenger and Jenae Thompson

Example 1

Teaching Philosophy

Caughlin (2014) stressed the importance of educator self-reflection to explore the logic behind why we conduct our classrooms, and ourselves as educators, in a particular manner. This self-reflection should then be made available to students in the form of a teaching philosophy, which will provide students with insight into our teaching methods (Caughlin, 2014). The following will explore my goals for student learning, how I plan to approach these goals in the classroom, and finally how the attainment of these goals will be measured. From the spirit of constructivism (as well as a Rogerian person-centered perspective), I view myself as a mentor or guide to my students as opposed to the "sage on the stage" or the expert. By taking this collaborative stance, I insist upon my students reflecting on their own knowledge—both within the course and outside of it—to help them become responsible for their growth as adult learners.

Goals for Student Learning

In order to succeed in a counselor education program, students should possess a variety of professional, personal, and academic traits. Student motivation is a difficult concept to conceptualize, but it is absolutely vital to student success in not only a counseling program but in the broader classroom of academia (Gom, 2009). Successful students will be self-aware of their motivators, both intrinsic and extrinsic, and will draw on this motivation to keep them focused throughout the program (Gom, 2009; McKeachie & Svinicki, 2014). Effective instructors will foster a learning environment where motivation and self-reliance are encouraged, therefore increasing students' dependence on their own initiative (McCaughan, Binkley, Wilde, Parmanand, & Allen, 2013).

Successful students will possess the coping strategies necessary to appropriately manage any self-doubt or excessive worry that may occur as a result of feeling unsure of their developing skill sets (Aladag, Yaka, & Koc, 2014; Jordan & Kelly, 2011). Although anxiety and nervousness are developmentally appropriate for counselors in training, an excess of either may inhibit the counselor's ability to succeed in the program and beyond in his work as a professional (Adalag et al., 2014). Through engagement in a counseling program, students should develop the self-awareness to monitor these reactions and also develop the self-care strategies needed to process them (Jordan & Kelly, 2011; Kerl, Garcia, McCullough, & Maxwell, 2002).

More than just content knowledge is necessary for success in the counseling profession (Kerl et al., 2002). Personal factors must be evaluated in addition to academic abilities and content knowledge (Lumadue & Duffey, 1999). Students must also demonstrate an ability to effectively form therapeutic relationships with clients, and additionally they must prove their ability to manage their own emotions and self-care so it does not interfere with the counseling relationship (Kerl et al., 2002).

A foundational level of knowledge of counseling theories, techniques, diagnosis, and other skills must be possessed for success as a professional counselor. Counselors in training must demonstrate their ability to synthesize a high volume of information (content knowledge as well as case information from the client) in order to accurately conceptualize the case and apply appropriate methods of treatment (Granello & Haag, 2000). Additionally, they must become adept at balancing the role of student, counselor in training, and individual if they are to succeed at their internship sites and beyond (Edwards & Patterson, 2012).

ROLE OF OBJECTIVES

The role of learning objectives in student learning is to provide a rationale for the purpose of the course content (Gambescia, 2006; West, Bubenzer, Cox, & McGlothin, 2013). The presence of objectives creates consistent expectations for both the faculty teaching the course as well as the student taking the course, as they are both responsible for meeting the objectives (West et al., 2013). Objectives specify for students what knowledge they will gain through participation in a course and also how they will be expected to utilize that information (Granello, 2001). This is typically done by utilizing language from Bloom's Taxonomy within the objectives to indicate how information will be expected to be used (Granello, 2001).

Although there will be variations from course to course, the learning objectives across my courses will require students to demonstrate higher order thinking (Bissell & Lemons, 2006; Granello, 2001). Skills such as application, synthesis, and evaluation require the highest levels of critical thinking and understanding, and therefore would be necessary to demonstrate thorough understanding of course materials (Granello, 2001). The diverse backgrounds of students in the classroom may require me to assist them with gaining an understanding of how to achieve the learning objectives, as some cultures may view evaluation, for example, as questioning of authority (Chuang, 2012). Ford, Stuart, and Vakil (2014) cautioned educators to not to adjust expectations, but rather be flexible with the methods of achieving those expectations to accommodate diverse learning approaches in the classroom.

BENEFITS OF COURSES

My goal for students will be that they receive more benefits from taking my courses than simply an understanding of the content knowledge. By the end of my courses, I want students to have developed a strong sense of intrinsic motivation to learn as well as an increased sense of self-reliance (Gom, 2009; McCaughan et al., 2013). Students should also improve their critical thinking and synthesis skills, as these are imperative to demonstrate a thorough understanding of content knowledge (Granello, 2001).

Enactment of Goals

TEACHING METHODS

Counselor educators should approach the classroom with a variety of strategies aimed toward facilitating the development of counseling students' personal and professional growth (Morrissette & Gadbois, 2006). This should include the encouragement of ongoing self-reflection to ensure students are engaging in self-care related to the appropriateness of participating in class activities (Morrissette & Gadbois, 2006). Additionally, delivery of course content will involve various experiential options to provide a diverse learning environment for students (Laureate Education, 2015). By incorporating hands-on, experiential learning opportunities, students are encouraged to take ownership over the depth of their learning allowing the educator to function as a guide rather than as the only source of knowledge in the classroom (Swank, 2012; Weigel & Bonica, 2014). Because experiential methods have been demonstrated to more positively contribute to student learning than lecture style methods, I believe their use will positively impact the goals I have for students' learning (Malott, Hall, Sheely-Moore, Krell, & Cardaciotto, 2014).

CONNECTION BETWEEN METHODS AND OBJECTIVES

Teaching methods should support learning objectives by providing opportunities for students to actively engage with class material and assess their
own understanding of the resources (Malott et al., 2014). Since my learning
objectives will require students to demonstrate higher order thinking skills
(application, synthesis, evaluation), the activities I utilize throughout the term
should provide students an opportunity to practice with these skills (Laureate
Education, 2015). Active engagement with class materials is positively associated with increased student motivation for learning, also, making experiential
activities an effective supplement no matter the specific learning objective
(Scott, 2012).

PREFERRED TEACHING METHODS

An effective educator will utilize a variety of instructional methods in order
to accommodate the range of learning styles present in their classrooms
(Cornelius, Gordon, & Ackland, 2011; McKeachie & Svinicki, 2014). My
personal preference is for leading discussions and group work activities, but
I appreciate the value of all teaching methods and recognize that lecture is
appropriate in many circumstances (Caughlin, 2014; West et al., 2013). Multiple
strategies of teaching should be used for each topic to assist students with
diverse learning styles and cultural backgrounds in absorbing the material
(McKeachie & Svinicki, 2014). Instructional technology can be a helpful support
in the classroom, as it again assists with making the material accessible to
students in multiple ways (Laureate Education, 2015). I will utilize PowerPoint
technology, videos, case vignettes, and other strategies to engage students
while carefully considering which approach will work best for the day's topic.

IMPLICATIONS OF SETTING ON TEACHING APPROACH

Educators must remain flexible in their teaching methods due to the large
impact setting can have on the usefulness of certain approaches. In a strictly
land-based environment, I imagine I would rely on hands-on experiences,
games, and group discussion opportunities to facilitate the learning of course
materials (Cornelius et al., 2011; Swank, 2012). Because of the flexibility
inherent in a land-based environment, I would be able to incorporate key
topics that emerge from students into the discussion, perhaps deviating
slightly from the planned lesson (Cornelius et al., 2011). I believe this type of
flexibility provides a model for students, as well, that effective learning can,
and should, expand from the lesson's learning resources. If I find myself
teaching in an online-only or hybrid counselor education program, I will have

to adjust my teaching strategies accordingly. Written communication, although always important, becomes even more important in an online teaching setting since it is the main form of communication with students.

Assessment of Goals

It is important for educators to assess student learning on an ongoing basis, as this provides a measurement of not only how well students are learning but also of the effectiveness of an educator's teaching methods (Baroudi, 2007). Throughout an individual course and a counseling program as a whole, students will be assessed for academic progress, clinical progress, and appropriateness for the profession (Hensley, Smith, & Thompson, 2003). There is a reciprocal relationship between an assessment measure and the curriculum of courses within a counseling program; the curriculum of the course should guide the development of the assessment and the assessment should help to troubleshoot for whether all elements of the curriculum are being covered effectively (Daugherty, Black, Ecclestone, James, & Newton, 2008).

METHODS OF ASSESSMENT

Rubrics are helpful tools for measuring student learning and performance (Andrade, 2005). They can be helpful measurement tools for assessing the performance of students on written assignments (Andrade, 2005; Bissell & Lemons, 2006). Additionally, rubrics can help to contextualize what higher order thinking skills will look like in practice (e.g., synthesis of sources, evaluation of information, etc.) as these can be difficult to define (Baroudi, 2007; Bissell & Lemons, 2006).

Because written assignments provide an opportunity for students to actively apply and synthesize the information learned in class, I will rely on them as one type of assignment in my courses (Granello, 2001). Tests and other memorization-focused assessment tools can be appropriate for some elements of course content, but they will not necessarily demonstrate a student's true understanding of class materials (Bissell & Lemons, 2006). A variety of opportunities for students to demonstrate their learning, as well as a variety of tools for measuring that learning, will help to provide a well-rounded demonstration of course performance (Baroudi, 2007).

Regardless of the assessment measure or type of assignment utilized, I would aim to encourage student-directed learning and an increasing reliance on their ability to self-monitor their learning by the end of the term (Baroudi,

2007). Student learning will be apparent when they are able to demonstrate self-direction and self-motivation toward meeting the goals of the course (Gom, 2009). As a course progresses, I want to reinforce the importance of assessments not as just grading tools, but more importantly as measures for determining how well and how thoroughly the students are learning; this shifts the focus from evaluation of learning to cultivation of a desire for learning (Baroudi, 2007).

THE ROLE OF STUDENT EVALUATIONS

Educators should utilize evaluation measures to determine how effective their teaching strategies have been throughout each course (Baroudi, 2007). Student evaluations of teaching and learning are one strategy for collecting this feedback. However, informal methods of gathering feedback, such as discussion and questioning, should be conducted throughout the course so changes can be made immediately if approaches are found to be ineffective (Scott, 2012). One informal strategy for garnering student feedback and assessing student learning could be the minute paper, completed at the end of each class session, which asks students to restate the most important information they learned that day (Smith-Adcock, Ropers-Huilman, & Choate, 2004). If multiple students fail to address what I felt was the main idea for the class session, I can determine that my methods were ineffective and will be able to immediately adjust the next class session to accommodate this deficit.

REMEDIATION APPROACH

In counseling programs, students must be assessed for content knowledge as well as the personal characteristics necessary for success as a professional counselor (Hensley et al., 2003). Some students may demonstrate a knowledge deficit. In those cases, I could utilize feedback to guide students toward the knowledge and skills necessary for growth (McKeachie & Svinicki, 2014). If students have continued difficulty in this area, recommendations for continuing education, supplemental assignments or reading, or even repeating a specific course may be required. Additionally, I should reflect on the manner in which I have been delivering information in class to ensure I am accommodating a variety of learning styles, since an absence of this could be negatively affecting the student's performance as well (McKeachie & Svinicki, 2014).

Another important consideration is whether the student possesses the personal and professional qualities necessary for success as a counselor (Daugherty, Coker, & Haddock, 2014). Because minor issues can turn into major concerns, or even tragedies, if not addressed in a timely fashion, it is imperative that counselor educators respond to concerns swiftly (Burkholder, Hall, & Burkholder, 2014; Harrell & Hollins, 2009). For students exhibiting behavioral concerns, I will utilize a remediation process which mirrors the counseling process (Wilkerson, 2006). The intake and evaluation would involve assessing the student's perception of the deficit as well as identifying appropriate resources and options for remediation (Wilkerson, 2006). If such informal methods of remediation are not sufficient, it may be necessary to engage in a more formal remediation process with the student (Kerl et al., 2002; Kress & Protivnak, 2009; Wilkerson, 2006).

GATEKEEPING

When informal methods of remediation are not sufficient, it may become necessary to engage a student in a formal remediation plan to address deficits in academic, professional, or personal development (Harrell & Hollins, 2009; Wilkerson, 2006; Ziomek-Daigle & Christensen, 2010). Gatekeeping involves a responsibility to the university, the profession, and to the counseling student individually (Kress & Protivnak, 2009). If the student is unable to reach minimal standards, dismissal from the program may be needed as part of the gatekeeping responsibility of counselor educators (McAdams & Foster, 2007).

Duties to the individual student include preventing those students lacking in the minimum standards for self-care from entering into the profession, as some students will lack the ability to appropriately manage the stress levels associated with such an emotionally demanding profession (Glance, Fanning, Schoepke, Soto, & Williams, 2012). With this in mind, gatekeeping can be in the best interest of the student as it would prevent him or her from entering a field for which they are unqualified (Glance et al., 2012). Duties to the university involve minimizing any potential liability involved with awarding an under-qualified student with a degree in counseling, as this could hold the university liable for the counselor's behaviors in the future (Burkholder et al., 2014). And finally, the American Counseling Association's Code of Ethics (2014) require counselor educators to minimize potential for harm to clients, which could involve dismissal of those students who are ill-suited for the profession.

Conclusion

The role of a counselor educator is complex as it involves obligations to the profession of counseling, the interests of the university, any potential clients, and finally the students in our classrooms. The preceding has discussed my philosophy of teaching and learning as well as how I will enact this philosophy in my future role as a counselor educator. As I shift into direct service as a counselor educator, I will continue to evolve in my beliefs, and therefore my philosophy of teaching and learning will continue to evolve as well.

References

American Counseling Association. (2014). *The 2014 ACA code of ethics*. Retrieved from www.counseling.org/Resources/aca-code-of-ethics.pdf.

Aladag, M., Yaka, B., & Koç, I. (2014). Opinions of counselor candidates regarding counseling skills training. *Educational Sciences: Theory and Practice, 14*(3), 879–886.

Andrade, H. G. (2005). Teaching with rubrics: The good, the bad, and the ugly. *College Teaching, 53*(1), 27–30.

Baroudi, Z. M. (2007). Formative assessment: Definition, elements and role in instructional practice. *Post-Script, 8*(1), 37–48.

Bissell, A. N., & Lemons, P. P. (2006). A new method for assessing critical thinking in the classroom. *Bioscience, 56*(1), 66–72

Burkholder, D., Hall, S. F., & Burkholder, J. (2014). Ward v. Wilbanks: Counselor educators respond. *Counselor Education and Supervision, 53*(4), 267–283.

Caughlin, D. (2014). Enhancing your teaching experience: Developing your teaching philosophy, course syllabus, and teaching portfolio. *The Industrial-Organizational Psychologist, 52*(2), 94–99. Retrieved from www.siop.org/tip/oct14/pdfs/TT.pdf.

Chuang, S. (2012). Different instructional preferences between western and Far East Asian adult learners: A case study of graduate students in the USA. *Instructional Science, 40* (3), 477–492.

Cornelius, S., Gordon, C., & Ackland, A. (2011). Towards flexible learning for adult learners in professional contexts: an activity-focused course design. *Interactive Learning Environments, 19*(4), 381–393. doi:10.1080/10494820903298258.

Daugherty, R., Black P., Ecclestone, K., James, M., & Newton, P. (2008). Alternative perspectives on learning outcomes: Challenges for assessment. *The Curriculum Journal, 19*(4), 243–254.

Dougherty, A., Coker, K., & Haddock, L. (2014). *An ethical examination of student development and remediation processes for counselors in training*. Paper presented at the ACES Conference, Denver, Colorado. Retrieved from www.counseling.org/docs/default-source/vistas/student-development-and-remediation-processes-for-counselors-in-training-in-a-virtual-environment.pdf?sfvrsn=4.

Edwards, T. M., & Patterson, J. E. (2012). The daily events and emotions of master's-level family therapy trainees in off-campus practicum settings. *Journal of Marital and Family Therapy, 38*(4), 688–696.

Ford, B. A., Stuart, D. H., & Vakil, S. (2014). Culturally responsive teaching in the 21st century inclusive classroom. *Journal of The International Association of Special Education, 15*(2), 56–62.

Gambescia, S. F. (2006). Syllabus construction with a commitment to shared governance. *Journal of Continuing Higher Education, 54*(1), 20–27.

Glance, D., Fanning, G., Schoepke, A., Soto, W., & Williams, M.A. (2012). *Gatekeeping in counselor education*. Retrieved from www.counseling.org/docs/default-source/vistas/vistas_2012_article_11.

Gom, O. (2009). Motivation and adult learning. *Contemporary PNG Studies: DWU Research Journal, 10,* 17–25. Retrieved from www.dwu.ac.pg/en/images/Research_Journal/2009_Vol_10/2_Gom_17-25_Motivation__Adult_Learning.pdf.

Granello, D. H. (2001). Promoting cognitive complexity in graduate written work: Using Bloom's taxonomy as a pedagogical tool to improve literature reviews. Counselor *Education & Supervision, 40*(4), 292

Granello, D. H., & Haag, D. (2000). Encouraging the cognitive development of supervisees: Using Bloom's taxonomy in supervision. *Counselor Education and Supervision, 40*(1), 31–46.

Harrell II, I. L., & Hollins, Jr., T. N. (2009). Working with disruptive students. *Inquiry, 14*(1), 69–75. Retrieved from http://files.eric.ed.gov/fulltext/EJ833920.pdf.

Hensley, L. G., Smith, S. L., & Thompson, R. W. (2003). Assessing competencies of counselors in-training: complexities in evaluating personal and professional development. *Counselor Education and Supervision, 42*(3), 219–230.

Jordan, K., & Kelly, W. E. (2011). A preliminary factor analytic investigation of beginning counseling students' worries. *Psychology Journal, 8*(1), 2–10.

Kerl, S B., Garcia, J. L., McCullough, C. S., & Maxwell, M. E. (2002). Systematic evaluation of professional performance: Legally supported procedure and process. *Counselor Education and Supervision, 41*(4), 321–332.

Knowles, M. S., Holton, III, E. F., & Swanson, R. A. (2005). *Adult learner: The definitive classic in adult education and human resources development* (6th ed.). Burlington, MA: Elsevier.

Kress, V. E., & Protivnak, J. J. (2009). Professional development plans to remedy problematic counseling student behaviors. *Counselor Education and Supervision, 48*(3), 154–166.

Laureate Education (Producer). (2015). *Teaching in counselor education: Acquisition of knowledge and skills* [Video file]. Baltimore, MD: Author.

Lumadue, C. A., & Duffey, T. H. (1999). The role of graduate programs as gatekeepers: A model for evaluating student counselor competence. *Counselor Education and Supervision, 39*(2), 101–109.

Malott, K. M., Hall, K. H., Sheely-Moore, A., Krell, M. M., & Cardaciotto, L. (2014). Evidence based teaching in higher education: Application to counselor education. *Counselor Education and Supervision, 53*(4), 294–305.

McAdams, C. R., & Foster, V. A. (2007). A guide to just and fair remediation of counseling students with professional performance deficiencies. *Counselor Education and Supervision, 47*(1), 2–13.

McCaughan, A., Binkley, E., Wilde, B., Parmanand, S., & Allen, V. (2013). Observing the development of constructivist pedagogy in one counselor education doctoral cohort: A single case design. *The Practitioner Scholar: Journal of Counseling and Professional Psychology, 2*(1), 95–108.

McKeachie, W., & Svinicki, M. (2014). *McKeachie's teaching tips: Strategies, research, and theory for college and university teacher* (14th ed.). Independence, KY: Cengage Learning.

Morrissette, J., & Gadbois, S. (2006). Ethical consideration of counselor education teaching strategies. *Counseling and Values, 50*(2), 131–141.

Scott, S. J. (2012). Constructivist perspectives for developing and implementing lesson plans in general music. *General Music Today, 25*(2), 24–30. doi:10.1177/1048371311398285

Smith-Adcock, S., Ropers-Huilman, B., & Choate, L. H. (2004). Feminist teaching in counselor education: Promoting multicultural understanding. *Journal of Multicultural Counseling & Development, 32*, 402–413.

Swank, J. M. (2012). Using games to creatively enhance the counselor education curriculum. *Journal of Creativity in Mental Health, 7*(4), 397–340. doi:10.1080/15401383.2012.740365

Weigel, F. K., & Bonica, M. (2014). An active learning approach to Bloom's taxonomy: 2 games, 2 classrooms, 2 methods. *U.S. Army Medical Department Journal*, 21–29.

West, J. D., Bubenzer, D. L., Cox, J. A., & McGlothin, J. M. (Eds). (2013). *Teaching in Counselor Education: Engaging Students*. Alexandria, VA: American Counseling Association.

Wilkerson, K. (2006). Impaired students: Applying the therapeutic process model to graduate training programs. *Counselor Education and Supervision, 45*(3), 207–217.

Ziomek-Daigle, J., & Christensen, T. M. (2010). An emergent theory of gatekeeping practices in counselor education. *Journal of Counseling and Development, 88*(4), 407–415.

Example 2

Personal Teaching Philosophy

As I look back on my time in this Counselor Education and Supervision (CES) program, I am reminded of how much I have grown over the last three years. Over the last three months, I have reflected on my personal and professional goals and have come to realize how they are synonymous. Through this program, I have learned how much my self-direction has helped me grow professionally and personally. As an adult learner completing a degree online I have relied heavily on self-reflection and critical thinking to guide and motivate me to continue (Brookfield, 1986). The majority of interactions have been asynchronous but because of my interest and motivation to learn and create relationships, I have found several people who have supported me and I also support to complete this program. I will continue to fine-tune my pedagogical identity. In this post, I will discuss how my teaching philosophy has transformed since the last quarter including my updated pedagogical philosophy, analyze a peer's teaching philosophy, and then I will analyze how I will apply this philosophy and pedagogy to both traditional educational and online settings.

Personal Pedagogical Identity

Relational Cultural Theory (RCT) as a pedagogy is in its formative years. Currently, there are increasing amounts of information supporting its use in the counseling field and educators preparing primary and secondary school teachers and social workers are advocating that it be utilized by instructors in the classroom (Buck, Mast, Lattab, & Kaftan, 2009; Edwards & Richards, 2002; Walker, 2015; Wang, 2012). Relational Cultural Theory as a pedagogy emphasizes the need to move beyond constructs when educating others (Edwards and Richards, 2002). Relational-Cultural Theory utilizes a growth-fostering perspective appropriate for all stages of professional development (Duffey, Haberstroh, Ciepcielinski, & Gonzales, 2016).

My personal attraction to this theory is due to the natural aspects of learning that connect people to each other despite the differences experienced between them. Relational knowing connects students to teachers and subject matter in a manner that does not aggressively control the learning experience for all involved (Buck, et al., 2009). Rather, the learning experience involves an organic process that places emphasis on the existential location of one's self in relationship to others and information shared (Buck et al., 2009). The concept of location of self is also discussed in the theory of intersectionality, a theory that places emphasis on the personal agency in the learning experience (Brown, Collins, Arthur, 2014; Watts-Jones, 2010).

Evaluation of a Different Teaching Philosophy

An esteemed colleague and CES faculty mentor utilizes constructivism as theory teaching philosophy and pedagogical approach. As a pedagogical tool, constructivism allows faculty to encourage problem-solving and critical thinking skills by promoting exploration of alternates (Eriksen & McAuliffe, 2001). Similar to RCT as a pedagogical tool, constructivism allows faculty to promote experiential learning, reflection, and metacognition (Eriksen & McAuliffe, 2001; Wang, 2012). Constructivism allows faculty to construct training experiences that model the value of experience, active learning, and reflective practice all of which are imperative in formulating productive learning environments and sustainable relationships (Eriksen & McAuliffe, 2001).

In this way, constructivism allows faculty members to perform many of the components that are necessary for RCT, including understanding one's social location in relationship to the learning environment, on the backend (Brown, Collins, & Arthur, 2014; Watts-Jones, 2010).

Influence of Pedagogy on Traditional and Online Settings

My teaching experience includes guest lecturing and currently participating as a teaching assistant with Walden University for internship. I have limited formal experience teaching at traditional institutions, but the application of engagement in traditional settings using RCT has proven effective due to mutual empowerment (Edwards & Richards, 2002; Walker & Rosen, 2004). Rather than focusing on maintaining the hierarchy in the relationship between faculty and student, RCT encourages mutual empowerment, which teaches students the importance of non-hierarchical relationships and decreases the likelihood of humiliation (Edwards & Richards, 2002). There is limited information available about the use of RCT in an online setting; however, the implications for applying it virtually should be no different than applying it traditionally.

Attention to details regarding intention and perception of tone, inflection, and pitch with asynchronous communication vs. synchronous communication is imperative for any type of educational setting, but especially online (Trepal, Haberstroh, Duffey, & Evans, 2007). In my experience with my teaching assistantship last quarter and again this quarter, I recognize the need for supportive responses, rather than defensive ones, and open dialogue that supports students so they can learn to accept feedback. Neden and Burnham (2007) discussed the concept of relational reflexivity as a way to teach counseling students how to conduct family therapy. Relational reflexivity is the knowledge counselors gain and need to be successful through generative and collective interactions with others (Neden & Burnham, 2007). I hope to continue practicing my own reflexive processes to ensure coherence and congruence no matter the setting I teach.

Transformation

As a counselor, educator, and supervisor, I have developed relationships and acquired tools which have allowed me to contribute to this field in ways I did not think possible before completing a doctoral degree. Despite these experiences, I do not see the achievement of completing this degree as the end of my professional pursuits. My desire to learn and grow extends beyond this program even as an educator. I think my pedagogical identity has supported this evolution and I am looking forward to seeing where it takes me next.

References

American Counseling Association. (2014). *The 2014 ACA code of ethics*. Retrieved from www.counseling.org/Resources/aca-code-of-ethics.pdf.

Brookfield, S. D. (1986). *Understanding and facilitating adult learning*. San Francisco, CA: Jossey-Bass.

Brown, C. B., Collins, S., & Arthur, N. (2014). Fostering multicultural and social justice competence through counsellor education pedagogy. *Canadian Journal of Counseling and Psychotherapy, 48*(3), 300–320.

Buck, G. A., Mast, C. M., Lattab, M. M., & Kaftan, J. M. (2009). Fostering a theoretical and practical understanding of teaching as a relational process: A feminist participatory study of mentoring a doctoral student. *Educational Action Research, 17*(4), 505–521. doi:10.1080/09650790903309375.

Duffey, T., Haberstroh, S., Ciepcielinski, E., & Gonzales, C. (2016). Relational_cultural theory and supervision: Evaluating developmental relational counseling. *Journal of Counseling and Development, 94*(4), 405–414. doi:10.1002/jcad.12099.

Edwards, J. B., & Richards, A. (2002). Relational teaching: A view of relational teaching in social work education. *Journal of Teaching in Social Work, 22*(1/2), 33.

Eriksen, K, & McAuliffe, G. (2001). *Teaching counselors and therapists: Constructivist and developmental course design*. Westport, CT: Bergin & Garvey.

Neden, J., & Burnham, J. (2007). Using relational reflexivity as a resource in teaching family therapy. *Journal of Family Therapy, 29*(4), 359–363. doi:10.1111/j.1467-6427.2007.00402.x.

Trepal, H., Haberstroh, S., Duffey, T., & Evans, M. (2007). Considerations and strategies for teaching online counseling skills: Establishing relationships in cyberspace. *Counselor Education and Supervision, 46*(4), 266–279. doi:10.1002/j.1556-6978.2007.tb00031.x.

Walker, M., & Rosen, W. B. (Eds). (2004). *How connections heal: Stories from relational-cultural therapy*. New York, NY: Guildford Press.

Walker, S. (2015). Relationship-based teaching: A relational ethics led approach to teaching social work. *Ethics and Social Welfare, 9*(4), 394–402. doi:10.1080/1749 6535.2015.1088703.

Wang, D. (2012). The use of self and reflective practice in relational teaching and adult learning: A social work perspective. *Reflective Practice, 13*(1), 55–63. doi:10.1080/ 14623943.2011.616887.

Watts-Jones, T. (2010). Location of self: Opening the door to dialogue on inter-sectionality in the therapy process. *Family and Practice, 43*(3), 256–264.

Teaching Philosophy Self-Reflection

Laura R. Haddock

As you conclude your introduction to the role of teaching for counselor educators, you will now begin development of your own teaching philosophy. You have been exposed to a broad overview of the roles of counselor educators and the responsibilities of those who train future clinicians. Review the following list of common evaluation components which faculty members are typically assessed on annually. Note the areas that stand out to you as needing the most attention in your own development, so you can keep these in mind as you move forward in your professional identity development.

- Are the teaching activities appropriate to the achievement of the established learning goals and objectives?
- Have **you** set rigorous and appropriate, course-specific learning goals and measurable outcomes and are they clearly communicated to students (e.g. in the syllabus)?
- Have you chosen course assignments, learning activities and assessments that enable students to meet the course's stated learning outcomes?
- **Do you** provide evidence of an intellectual understanding of, and engagement in, the continual process of reflection on, and improvement of, teaching?
- Does course content reflect current scholarship in the field?
- Are course syllabi, outlines, and/or any other materials for course use well-constructed, detailed, and informative and are they reviewed and revised regularly?
- Do you demonstrate a broad repertoire of pedagogical strategies and show evidence of knowing when and how to use different strategies?
- Do you demonstrate the use of appropriate and various pedagogical and instructional techniques to maximize student learning and the use of innovative approaches?

Quiz

1. Which is a major principle of andragogy?

   a. Adults need to know why they need to learn something
   b. Adults expect their experiences to be valued
   c. Adults expect to be directed by their professors
   d. Adults are motivated by rewards for learning
   e. A and B
   f. A and D

2. A good teaching philosophy normally includes not just who you are as a professor but who the students are as learners as well:

   a. True
   b. False

3. Feminist pedagogy is usually included in which learning theory:

   a Constructivism
   b. Critical Pedagogy
   c. Transformative Learning

4. Brain-based learning encompasses the following concepts:

   a. Experiential and collaborative learning
   b. Parallel processing
   c. Self-reflection
   d. Experiential learning
   e. All of the above

5. At a minimum, a teaching philosophy should address all but:

   a. Goals of learning
   b. Assessment of your teaching
   c. Connection to your research
   d. Diversity of learners and learning styles

6. Problem-based learning includes the following steps:

   a. Synthesis of new learning
   b. Independent inquiry
   c. Problem-definition
   d. Group formation
   e. All of the above

7. According to one study on the connection of neuroscience to educational outcomes, which of the following were not features of excellent educators?

   a. Creativity
   b. Dynamism
   c. Concentration
   d. Rigor

8. Frame of reference is a term most closely associated with which learning theory?

   a. Transformative Learning Theory
   b. Problem Based Learning
   c. Critical Pedagogy
   d. Constructivism

9. Research on teaching philosophy statements suggests that a good statement is one that is based on a teaching philosophy boilerplate:

   a. True
   b. False

10. In addition to including the theory of learning you ascribe to, it is important to also include:

   a. Your counseling theoretical orientation
   b. Examples of how you teach
   c. Behaviors of effective learning
   d. How you assess learning
   e. All but C

11. Constructivist theorists believe there is no one truth and that knowledge is co-created between learner and teacher:

   a. True
   b. False

12. Knowles, Holton, and Swanson (2005) recommended an eight-step process for instructing learners that includes all but:

   a. Preparing the learner
   b. Establishing a climate conducive to learning
   c. Formulating program objectives
   d. Evaluating the learning outcomes and deciding what you believe the learner needs

13. In Problem Based Learning, the problem-scenario is crafted from a student's definition:

    a. True
    b. False

14. Which theory of learning is most concerned with social justice?

    a. Constructivism
    b. Critical Pedagogy
    c. Problem-Based Learning
    d. Transformative Learning Theory

15. Malott, Hall, Sheely-Moore, Krell, and Cardaciotto (2014) recommend three foci for best practices when crafting a teaching philosophy. They include attention to all but:

    a. How you create an effective learning environment
    b. How you develop learning outcomes
    c. How you structure intentional learning experiences
    d. How you assess for effective teaching

3 Ethical and Legal Issues for Counselor Educators

Knowledge of counseling professional ethics and federal laws is mandatory for successful teaching. This chapter will provide experiential exercises to deepen understanding of ethical and legal issues related to teaching and being a gatekeeper for the profession. It will include:

- Case Studies of ethical and legal issues

- Managing resistance to feedback concerning ethical and legal behavior

- Quiz

Case Studies of Ethical and Legal Issues

Jenae Thompson

Case 1

Mark is a 68-year-old counselor educator. He has been working as a faculty member at a CACREP accredited institution since 1995 and is currently the department chair. Mark has not been successful with implementing necessary changes and updates to the on-site clinic. The clinic is used by Master's students for part of their practicum requirements in which they have some of their first clinical counseling experiences with clients from the local community. Some of the necessary changes and updates that Mark has not acquired for the clinic include digital storage of videos, emergency call buttons for each clinic room, and an adequate waiting room with a secretary. Mark has put off applying for grants that would help with the financial costs of the update to the clinic by stating that he does not think "you need to fix what isn't broken." Currently, the clinic uses VHS tapes to record the sessions and often when students bring them to supervision class, the quality of the tapes, which have been frequently reused, are poor.

1. What are some of the legal and ethical ramifications for this particular case?
2. How could Mark's lack of immediacy in response to the updates hinder the program's CACREP renewal?
3. How could cost-effective discussions about the electronic updates for the clinic further encourage a change to benefit this program?
4. As a colleague, how would you address the issue with Mark and with the chair of your department?

Case 2

You are in your first position as a counselor educator in a doctoral counselor education and supervision program. You are assigned to teach the course on qualitative research and have had one class in this subject in your doctoral program and identify more with an approach toward research that is quantitative by design. In fact, you found your qualitative research method and design class interesting yet questioned the rigor of qualitative approaches. You do not feel comfortable letting the Chair of the department know about your experience and interest in the subject, and yet you know you will be evaluated on your ability to teach this course effectively.

1. What are the ethical issues presented in this scenario?
2. How would you handle this ethical issue if it were you?
3. Who might you consult with before addressing the Chair?

Managing Resistance to Feedback Concerning Ethical and Legal Behavior

Joy S. Whitman

There will be ample opportunities to help students reflect on their behavior when it is focused on ethical and legal concerns. Students often flounder when their behavior borders on what is unethical more than what is illegal because of the nuanced character of ethics. To that end, here are case examples with guiding questions to help you consider how to manage resistance to feedback concerning ethical issues.

Case 1

Anita is a master's student in her practicum. She is eager to see clients and take on the "hard" cases. She is in your practicum class where you supervise a cohort of six students. During the third week of the term, she presents a case of a client with severe childhood trauma and adult dissociation. You are aware that Anita does not have the skill to ethically serve this client, yet Anita is not concerned as this is "just the kind of hard case I was hoping for." The other students in the class look to you because they are alarmed as well. You ask Anita about being assigned to this case, and she lets you know her supervisor said it was okay, that she would be there supervising her. You are even more concerned that her supervisor does not consider this client to be beyond Anita's knowledge and skill set and plan to speak to the supervisor. However, you first decide to speak to Anita after class to more clearly let her know of your concern. When you meet, Anita does not understand your worry and is thinks you do not believe in her ability and will question her supervisor as well. Though you clearly outline why you are concerned, she leaves the meeting feeling misunderstood and undermined.

- What are some ways you could discuss this with Anita? What are specific ways to communicate the ethical issues at hand?
- How can you use what you know about offering feedback to let her know you are not questioning her skill overall and are concerned ethically about this specific case?
- How can you assess her Anita's ability to manage feedback in general? What might you do to help her understand the ethical consequences of her behavior?

Case 2

You are a counselor educator in a doctoral program. You are assigned a teaching assistant (TA) to help you with one of your classes. You have worked with and mentored TAs in the past and are looking forward to doing so again. Louis, your TA, is excited to work with you and to start teaching with you. You meet to discuss your various roles with an eye toward easing Louis into the role of assessment of student assignments with your final approval of all feedback and grades assigned. It is clear Louis is pleased to be eased into this role, and you set up parameters between you about the process.

However, once Louis starts to grade students' work, you notice his feedback is harsh, critical, and non-supportive. When you speak with him about his tone, he says "I just can't believe how poorly these students write and how they are not learning the material. I do not want to go easy on them so they can learn." You discuss this with him and review how to effectively offer feedback. He seems open to your feedback as you model with him how to do so. Yet, you learn from an email a student in your class sends you that Louis contacted her to let her know that he thinks she is not integrating the feedback he is offering and that she is teetering on not passing the course. You speak to Louis who says, "What is the good in coddling these students? They have to learn this before they can work with clients. It is my ethical obligation to be a good gatekeeper."

- What are the ethical issues here?
- How can you continue to model how to offer effective feedback so Louis can integrate this behavior into his style?
- What are some ways you can give him feedback? How can you communicate the ethical concerns of his behavior with the student he emailed?
- How can you relay the importance of his behavior with you?

Quiz

1. Best practice for a counselor educator

   a. is the best professional behavior a counselor educator might be capable of achieving.
   b. occurs when a counselor educator strictly adheres to the ACA Code of Ethics.
   c. is the minimum behavior that society will tolerate from a counselor educator.
   d. is the behavior that a counselor educator exhibits who is practicing within legal standards.

2. When a student appeals a grade or dismissal, counselor educators are required to

   a. hold a hearing with attorneys present.
   b. include the following steps in grade or dismissal appeals: a written appeal from the student must be considered by a panel of faculty members, and if the student is dissatisfied with the result, the student is entitled to a formal hearing before the dean of the college.
   c. follow formal procedures that have been established that allow students to appeal.
   d. change grades or dismissal decisions if a student panel decides the grade or decision was unfair.

3. Gatekeeping can be exercised by counselor educators by taking any of the following actions EXCEPT

   a. denying an applicant admission to a counseling graduate program.
   b. not allowing a student to register for a course.
   c. assigning an unacceptable grade to a student in a required course.
   d. dismissing a student from a program.

4. The CACREP accreditation standards (2014) requires that programs demonstrate that students while enrolled in practicum and internship

   a. have professional liability insurance.
   b. have joined the American Counseling Association and have the free professional liability insurance provided by ACA.
   c. have professional liability insurance provided through their renters or homeowners insurance policy.
   d. have been encouraged to purchase professional liability insurance.

5. The ACA Code of Ethics (2014) defines plagiarism as

    a. failing to put in quotation marks direct quotes written by others.
    b. presenting another's work as your own.
    c. using at least 15 words written by another person without giving that other person credit.
    d. failing to provide an APA style reference after quoting another person's work.

6. When universities dismiss students who fail to meet the standards for clinical performance set by the university faculty, courts usually

    a. require university faculty to demonstrate that their standards are based on scientific evidence.
    b. reverse student dismissals.
    c. compare university standards to standards that have been found to be acceptable throughout the United States.
    d. defer to university professors in setting and evaluating standards for clinical performance.

7. When counselors are at risk of imposing their values onto clients, especially when the counselor's values are inconsistent with the client's goals or are discriminatory in nature, the ACA Code of Ethics (2014) requires that counselors

    a. refer clients to another counselor.
    b. seek training.
    c. consult with a counselor educator or supervisor.
    d. engage in self-reflection.

8. If a counseling graduate program graduate who a faculty member believes is not qualified for a credential or job requests an endorsement or recommendation from the faculty member, the best response for the faculty member would be to

    a. write a vague endorsement or letter to avoid upsetting the graduate.
    b. refuse to provide the endorsement or recommendation, but do not give reasons why.
    c. refuse to provide the endorsement or recommendation and explain to the graduate specific reasons for refusing.
    d. provide the endorsement or recommendation, but list any concerns about the student.

9. When supervisees are unable to demonstrate that they can provide competent professional services to a range of diverse clients, the ACA Code of Ethics says that supervisors should

    a. require supervisees to complete additional courses in ethics.
    b. recommend dismissal.
    c. assign counseling clients to the supervisees with whom the supervisee is comfortable providing services.
    d. put the supervisees on probation.

10. Which of the following were mentioned in Chapter 3 as an important piece of legislation relating to the education of people with disabilities?

    a. Americans with Disabilities Act (ADA).
    b. Section 504 of the Rehabilitation Act of 1973.
    c. Individuals with Disabilities Education Act (IDEA).
    d. all of the above.

11. All of the following were identified in Chapter 3 as examples of problematic student behaviors and dispositions EXCEPT

    a. clinical competence.
    b. inadequate interpersonal skills.
    c. difficulty regulating emotions.
    d. lack of initiative.

12. According to the 2016 CACREP Standards, all of the following should be included in student handbooks EXCEPT

    a. mission statement of the academic unit.
    b. information about professional counseling organizations.
    c. mentoring policy.
    d. academic appeal policy.

13. Counselor educators are encouraged to consult with _____ during the development of policies and procedures related to student remediation and dismissal.

    a. friends.
    b. students.
    c. legal representatives at their institution.
    d. licensed professional counselors.

14. CACREP (2016) requires that all of the following are included in course syllabi EXCEPT _____.

    a. content areas.
    b. names and contact information for program faculty.
    c. method of instruction.
    d. disability accommodation policy and procedure statement.

15. Counselor educators are responsible for which of the following in regards to assessment and evaluation?

    a. assessment of student learning.
    b. student evaluation of instructors and supervisors.
    c. program evaluation.
    d. all of the above.

4 Multicultural and Social Justice Leadership and Learning in the Classroom

Awareness of one's own cultural and diverse identities as well as those of one's students is significant for counselor educators and their development. This chapter offers supplemental materials to assist building insight and promoting self-awareness related to the role of cultural identity in the classroom and as part of the learning process. It will include consideration for the cultural identity of the teacher and the students. Activities will compromise of:

- Reflective exercise to enhance self-awareness related to cultural awareness and macroaggressions

- Exploring implicit bias

- Case study and process questions

- Guided questions to explore cultural misunderstanding and biases in teaching

- Quiz

Reflective Exercise to Enhance Self-Awareness Related to Cultural Awareness and Macroaggressions

Jenae Thompson

It is important for counselor educators to incorporate the foundational principles of intersectionality, including privilege and oppression, into their pedagogy. The following activity is a reflective journal that counselor education and supervision students and faculty can use as a guide throughout their career.

Reflective Journal Prompts

- What are your personal feelings (including self-resistance and affinity) toward diverse marginalized and privileged social groups/identities?
- In what ways are you working to increase your empathy with the marginalized and privileged groups you listed above?

  - What intrapersonal activities are you participating in?
  - What interpersonal activities are you participating in?

- How will increased empathy with the groups listed above improve your competency as a Counselor Educator and Supervisor?
- What are your multicultural and diversity goals as a Counselor Educator and Supervisor?

Exploring Implicit Bias

Laura R. Haddock

In order to take a more personal look at your own potential bias, take the Implicit Association test, which is available for free at https://implicit.harvard.edu/implicit/. Click on PROJECT IMPLICIT SOCIAL ATTITUDES.

Once you complete the assessment, consider the following questions:

- Were you surprised by your results?
- What did you learn about your perceptions of different social groups?
- How might these perceptions influence the way you approach teaching or supervising particular students?

- How do your own life experiences influence your approach to or avoidance of certain topics?
- What implications might this have for your work as a counselor educator?
- What strategies might you employ to avoid blind spots about your own bias?
- What is one way you can commit to a path of personal growth related to cultural awareness?

Case Study and Process Questions

Jenae Thompson

Brooke is a first-year counselor educator at a CACREP accredited institution teaching the multicultural counseling class. She is a 35-year-old White cisgender female. She has noticed that the class, which sits in rows, is divided into two sides, males and females. She has hit a stalemate with building rapport with all of the students; most of the male students talk over her and the female students, especially women of color, do not engage at all. Brooke brought this to the attention of her colleagues for feedback asking what she could do to create a more egalitarian learning environment for the class. She decided to have the class sit in a large circle, where she joined them, rather than having them all face her. She found this to lessen the interruptions, but the female students, especially women of color, continued to not engage as often as she would like.

Process Questions

- What other strategies might you employ if this were your class?
- For those students who are not engaging, how do you imagine they are acting in class and how might you engage them?
- What might Brooke be doing to create this scenario?
- How do the race and gender of the faculty member and students potentially lend explanation about the different dynamics presented in the case study?

Guided Questions to Explore Cultural Misunderstanding and Biases in Teaching

Jenae Thompson

- What are your personal and professional experiences with privilege and oppression? Provide examples.
- How have these experiences shaped your pedagogy or imagine they will?
- What role do you think your personal and professional experiences with privilege and oppression and those of your students should play in the classroom?
- How will you be aware of your experiences with privilege and oppression and work toward creating a learning environment where students can talk about their experiences?
- How will you help students explore their own experiences with privilege and oppression?

Quiz

1. Diversity is:

   a. not included in the counseling profession
   b. just recently included in the counseling profession
   c. has had a long history within the counseling profession
   d. none of the above

2. Diversity, Multiculturalism, and Social Justice are:

   a. interrelated
   b. separate concepts
   c. rooted in racial/ethnic concerns
   d. none of the above

3. Integral aspects of multicultural competence development include counselor:

   a. awareness
   b. knowledge
   c. skills
   d. all of the above

4. Social justice competence includes:

    a. counselor awareness, knowledge, and skills
    b. counselor awareness, knowledge, skills, and action
    c. privilege and oppression
    d. none of the above

5. Group dynamics are an important aspect of diversity in counselor education because:

    a. classrooms are a group
    b. there are different stages to groups that influence diversity learning
    c. setting the container of the class is related to exploring diversity
    d. all of the above

6. The following are important guiding documents related to diversity integration in counselor education:

    a. ACA Code of Ethics
    b. ACA Advocacy Competencies
    c. ACA Multicultural and Social Justice Competencies
    d. all of the above

7. When interacting with a student who is resistant to diversity training, you can:

    a. make them learn this dimension of training
    b. understand resistance is a normal part of learning diversity
    c. ignore them and focus on students who want to learn
    d. talk to your Dean before you speak with your faculty about the student

8. When building accountability for ongoing diversity training within your faculty, you can:

    a. integrate diversity into faculty meetings
    b. assess where faculty strengths and growing edges in diversity expertise are
    c. assess how diversity is integrated into various program activities
    d. all of the above

9. A self-exploration activity you can engage in with students explores the following areas:

   a. what people like and do not like
   b. social identity and related privilege and oppression
   c. what faculty think about diversity
   d. the ACA Ethics Code

10. Diversity should be integrated into all course content, and the following are helpful strategies to do so:

   a. self-disclosure and reflection as the instructor
   b. use of technology
   c. case studies
   d. all of the above

5 Classroom Engagement and Evidence-Based Teaching Strategies with Adult Learners

Adult learners and learners with varying learning styles require varied teaching strategies. Counselor educators must become familiar with evidence based and creative ways to engage the diverse learners they will teach. This chapter will provide activities designed to assist with the development of strategies to promote classroom engagement and evidence-based teaching and learning.

- Case studies and process questions focused on a mix of teaching strategies

- Guided questions to help integrate best practices in teaching and creativity for learning

- A collection of exercises to use in the classroom to promote engagement

- Quiz

Case Studies and Process Questions Focused on a Mix of Teaching Strategies

Sheila N. Russell

Case Study 1

Eileen Howard teaches a master's level course in a clinical and mental health program. Her students are expected to have read the material before coming to class each week. Eileen always opens her class by presenting a case study drawn from the course material the students were expected to have already read. Then she breaks them into breakout groups of three students per group so that the students can discuss the case of the day. She gives students about five minutes to discuss, then brings them back together as a whole group. She then asks a volunteer from each group to present to the whole class what their group discussed as a solution to the case study. After about three weeks of doing this, Eileen notices that the same students speak each week.

1. Assess the strategies that are effective and ineffective in this case. Rank the steps from least effective to most effective.
2. Identify what learning styles Eileen is using and which learning styles she has missed.
3. Develop strategies that Eileen should employ to ensure that all students are participating in the opening activity. Make sure you consider multiple learning styles.

Case Study 2

Eileen Howard then follows up the case study discussion with a mini lecture where she provides a summary of key concepts provided in the weekly material. The mini lecture is about 15 minutes long and she uses a visual during the lecture. After the mini lecture, students are given process questions to discuss. She will often split students into groups of two for them to discuss the process questions. Then, she brings them back as a whole group and calls on individual students to answer each question.

4. Identify the learning strategies Eileen is using in this case study. Which learning strategies is she not using? Develop a plan that would incorporate other learning strategies into Eileen's strategy.
5. Predict possible problems with Eileen's plan and develop solutions for those problems.

Case Study 3

At the end of each class, Eileen presents a summary the material that was covered for the day. She also briefly reviews upcoming assignments for the next week. Then, as the students leave the classroom, they must turn in a card that either identifies something the student learned that week or a question about the material. Eileen answers all questions in the online discussion board so that all students can see the question and her response.

6. Evaluate what works for you about this end of class strategy and what does not work for you. How would you change this technique to better fit your personal teaching philosophy and style?
7. How might you modify this teaching strategy for a classroom that does not have an online discussion board?
8. Create your own lesson plan using teaching strategies that incorporate multiple learning styles and that fit your own teaching style.

Guided Questions to Help Integrate Best Practices in Teaching and Creativity for Learning

Sheila N. Russell

The text offers you many opportunities to consider what are best practices in teaching and how to creatively help students learn. Below are some questions to further your reflective process as you develop your personal style of teaching.

- Identify the learning styles that your lesson incorporates. Are there any learning styles that you have not incorporated? Consider how you can redesign your lesson to incorporate these learning styles as well as those you have already included.

- Consider the arts when designing a lesson plan. How might you incorp-orate music, technology, or drawing? These skills allow students to use their own creativity to demonstrate mastery of a concept.
- Have you developed a lesson that allows students to move and discuss? If not, consider incorporating breakout sessions where students move around the room and discuss topics with their peers.
- What technology are you incorporating into your lesson? Have you considered multiple forms of technology such as discussion boards, chat rooms, videos, and synchronous polls? How might you add these platforms to a lesson to make the lesson more interesting?
- Have you developed an opening and closing for your lesson? Consider how you might "hook" students in the beginning of class and how you might check their understanding towards the end of class. Consider synchronous polls, a question of the day, or a case study that requires them to apply the information reviewed that day.
- Have you developed a rubric for grading assignments? Have you provided these rubrics to your students?

A Collection of Exercises to Use in the Classroom to Promote Engagement

Sheila N. Russell

In addition to the exercises in the text, below are a collection of additional exercises you can use. You are also invited to be creative and consider what each class' needs are and how you can organically create activities to fit their needs.

The Carousel Activity

The carousel activity is an interactive group activity that promotes movement and discussion among students. In the carousel activity, students are divided into groups. Then, a question, heading, topic, or theme is posed to each group. Each group has a few minutes to answer the question verbally or in writing. Groups then rotate in a circular, carousel fashion to the next comment, ques-tion, topic, theme, or heading. They then add to the previous answers with the new question. They cannot repeat what has already been stated in an answer. The activity continues until all the groups have rotated through each question.

KWL Chart

The KWL chart is used during the opening and closing of a lesson to check for previous knowledge and understanding. The K stands for "previous *knowledge* of the topic." The W stands for "*what* we hope to learn about the topic," and the L stands for "what we *learned* about the topic." Divide a chart into three columns. Label the first column K, the second column W, and the third column L. Then, at the opening of your lesson ask students what they already know about the concept or topic. Then, ask what they hope to learn about the concept or topic. At the end of your lesson, you can close by having students list what they learned about the concept or topic. Make sure you also check that you covered all the things listed in the L column. If you did not, this is an opportunity to extend the lesson outside of the classroom by having students research the answers to questions left unchecked. Have them report the answers at the beginning of the next class or by posting an online discussion post.

Synchronous Polls

Use synchronous polls in the classroom to check for previous knowledge or for understanding during or at the end of a lesson. Polls are a great way for students to come to class and immediately get engaged with the curriculum and content. There are many free poll websites and apps that are user friendly. One suggestion is to have a poll posted at the front of the room at the beginning of class as students walk in. You can pose an ethical question, present a case study, or ask a question specific to the course material. This is also an excellent way to make sure students are coming to class prepared.

Think-Pair-Share

Think-Pair-Share is a great activity to increase engagement in students who are too shy to speak out or need more time to process what they have learned. First, ask the entire class a question that they must first think about by themselves quietly. Then, they turn to a neighbor and discuss the question in pairs. Lastly, invite students to share their answers with the class.

3-2-1

The 3-2-1 activity is a great close activity to check for understanding. Students write three facts they learned about the material, two questions they still have about the topic, and one opinion they have about the topic. I like to have my students do this at the end of class. Then, I answer the most frequently asked questions in our online discussion board. Students can then continue their learning and engagement with the material outside of the classroom.

Fishbowl Role Play

A fish bowl role play is an activity used to role play counseling skills and techniques while requiring other students who are observers to remain engaged. Two students, one playing the counselor and one playing the client, sit in the middle of the classroom. The other students, or observers, sit in a circle surrounding the two students to make a fish bowl. The two students role play a counseling scenario. Then, the observers take turns telling the student playing the counselor one thing that worked for them and one thing that they would do differently. These comments can be specific to the concept or skill being taught. Then, the two students inside the fishbowl switch roles and the activity continues.

Quiz

1. How have scientists' understanding of the adult brain changed over time?

    a. Scientists now know the adult brain is inelastic and struggles learning new concepts
    b. Understanding of the adult brain has remained consistent
    c. Scientists found the adult brain more flexible and capable of adjusting to new information than previously believed
    d. The adult brain is larger and able to retain more information

2. In what way is learning considered a multidimensional process?

    a. Learning occurs in multiple levels of the brain
    b. Learning occurs differently depending on age, race, gender and culture
    c. Learning takes place in various contexts
    d. Learning encompasses brain, body and emotional well-being

3. Why are neural networks in adults more robust, and what are the implications?

   a. Their brains are bigger; they have more knowledge at their fingertips
   b. They have more experiences; their brains are more plastic
   c. They have more experiences; their brains are less plastic
   d. They have lived longer; it is easier to acquire a new skill

4. Which answer best describes the constructivist theory of learning?

   a. Creating meaning by connecting new information with past experiences
   b. Applying learning principles to one's behavior patterns
   c. Building learning capacity through movement
   d. Using patterns of thoughts to express oneself through constructing art

5. According to Bixby (2011), what is the cornerstone to teaching?

   a. Knowing all the answers
   b. Having an authoritative style with a strict class agenda
   c. Modeling vulnerability
   d. Having flexible office hours

6. What is the difference between learning style/preference and intelligence?

   a. Learning styles and preferences are fluid; intelligence can change
   b. Learning styles and preferences have to do with differences in ability; intelligence has to do with what activities you enjoy
   c. All three describe individual differences in learning
   d. Intelligence has to do with individual differences in ability, and learning styles/preferences do not

7. Which activity would be more likely to engage an adult learner, and why?

   a. A lecture and reading about a particular theorist, because adults like to soak up new information
   b. A case study, because emotion incites engagement and retention
   c. A group discussion, because all adults prefer group work
   d. None of the above

8. What is one limitation of research on learning styles?

   a. There is no concrete data to support it
   b. It doesn't exist

    c. It is impossible to research something so abstract

    d. There are no limitations

9. What is the "imposter syndrome"?

    a. Believing one is better than one's capabilities

    b. Feelings of not being as capable or adequate as others perceive or evaluate one to be

    c. Visualizing someone else in a professional role and mimicking that behavior

    d. Fear of public speaking and/or expression of one's views in a large group setting

10. Which choice best represents a parallel process your counseling students may NOT experience in Perry's stages?

    a. Feelings of being inadequate at a certain skill and being found out

    b. Dualistic ways of viewing the problem

    c. Being overwhelmed by multiple answers that all seem correct

    d. Overconfidence and emphasis on one's strengths without assessing for growth edges

11. Which of the below is NOT a viable strategy when working with adult students?

    a. Minimal feedback to create autonomy

    b. Group discussions and reflections

    c. Case studies

    d. Jigsaw

12. Which skill below would be most important for adult online learners?

    a. Technologically savvy

    b. Logical/Mathematical

    c. Autonomous

    d. Artistic

13. Gregorc's Mind Styles model includes:

    a. Concrete vs. abstract ways of perceiving information

    b. Sequential vs. random ways of processing information

    c. A quadrant-style theory

    d. All of the above

14. If a student displays strong preferences for brainstorming and learning by doing, according to Honey & Mumford s/he falls into the category of:

   a. Theorist
   b. Activist
   c. Pragmatist
   d. Reflector

15. Teamwork and group evaluation should:

   a. Incorporate multiple learning preferences and remain flexible
   b. Be random but have clear evaluative tools
   c. Maximize students' strengths and set clear and consistent metrics for group work
   d. Not be cultivated or encouraged in graduate programs due to the multiple demands students face

References

Bixby, D. W. (2011). Shut up and teach. *Talent Development*, (4), 32–34. Retrieved from: www.td.org/Publications/Magazines/TD.

Conaway, W., & Zorn-Arnold, B. (2015). The keys to online learning for adults: The six principles of andragogy. *Distance Learning*, 13(1), 1. Retrieved from: http://web.b.ebscohost.com/ehost/pdfviewer/pdfviewer?vid=1&sid=2b389e0a-d8f2-43 b3-9741-0ea3f3e63f37%40sessionmgr102.

Gardner, H. (1983). *Frames of mind: The theory of multiple intelligences*. New York, N.Y.: Basic Books.

Gregorc, A. F. (1984). *Gregorc style delineator: Development, technical and administration manual*. Gregorc Associates.

Hill, L. H. (2014). Graduate students' perspectives on effective teaching. *Adult Learning*, 25(2), 57–65. doi: 10.1177/1045159514522433.

Honey, P., & Mumford, A. (1986). *The manual of learning styles*. Peter Honey Associates.

Killen, R. (2007). *Effective teaching strategies: Lessons from research and practice*. (4th ed.). South Melbourne, Victoria: Thomson Social Science Press.

Moran, K., & Milsom, A. (2015). The flipped classroom in counselor education. *Counselor Education and Supervision*, 54(1), 32–43. doi: 10.1002/j.1556-6978.2015.00068.x.

Olusegun, S. (2015). Constructivism learning theory: A paradigm for teaching and learning. *Journal of Research & Method in Education*, 5(1), 66–70.

Pasher, H., McDaniel, M., Rohrer, D., & Bjork, R. (2008). Learning styles: Concepts and evidence. *Psychological Science in the Public Interest*, 9(3), 1–17. doi: 10.1111/j.1539-6053.2009.01038.x.

Perry, W. G. (1970). *Forms of intellectual and ethical development in the college years: A scheme*. New York: Holt, Rinehart and Winston.

Sakulku, J., & Alexander, J. (2011). The impostor phenomenon. *International Journal of Behavioral Science* (IJBS), 6(1). Retrieved from: http://ejournals.swu.ac.th/index.php/jbse/article/view/1712.

6 Acquisition of Knowledge and Skills

Case conceptualization exercises to deepen understanding of the process of developing and implementing learning objectives and accomplishing desired learning outcomes from students. This chapter will offer the following:

- Creating learning objectives using a template with Bloom's Taxonomy

- Examples of effective and ineffective learning objectives

- Connecting learning objectives to learning outcomes

- Quiz

Creating Learning Objectives Using a Template with Bloom's Taxonomy

Kristi Cannon

The process of developing a learning objective starts off with the objective itself—that is, what do we want the student to learn from the materials, resources, experiences provided? From that point we need to be able to determine how a student would actually demonstrate that they learned this information. Learning objectives allow us to do this.

One of the best ways to approach this complex task is to use a learning taxonomy. Bloom's Taxonomy of Cognitive Skills is a commonly used resource for classifying and writing student learning objectives, and was later revised to better integrate different types and levels of knowledge. This revised version of Bloom's taxonomy is most commonly used by educators today. A quick internet search will supply you with a myriad of support information and details specific to both Bloom's versions.

For the purposes of this activity here is what you need to know:

- Bloom's taxonomy is a series of metacognitive skills, where lower-level skills lay the foundation and where higher-order skills are scaffolded toward the top.
- From bottom to top, the skills are: Remember, Understand, Apply, Analyze, Evaluate, and Create
- Each skill level has a series of corresponding verbs that can be used to build your learning objective.
- The selection of level is specific to the goal of the learning and should be scaffolded based on prior learning.

Now, to build your learning objectives here are the steps to consider:

- What do I want students to learn through this activity?
- What prior learning or knowledge do they already have (i.e. too little and they will be easily frustrated and too much and they will find this redundant)?
- Based on this, which skill level should I be drawing from based on the Bloom's revised taxonomy?
- Using the Bloom's categories, which verb best reflects the action I want students to demonstrate?
- What are the details of the learning experience I explicitly want to see the students demonstrating through their action?

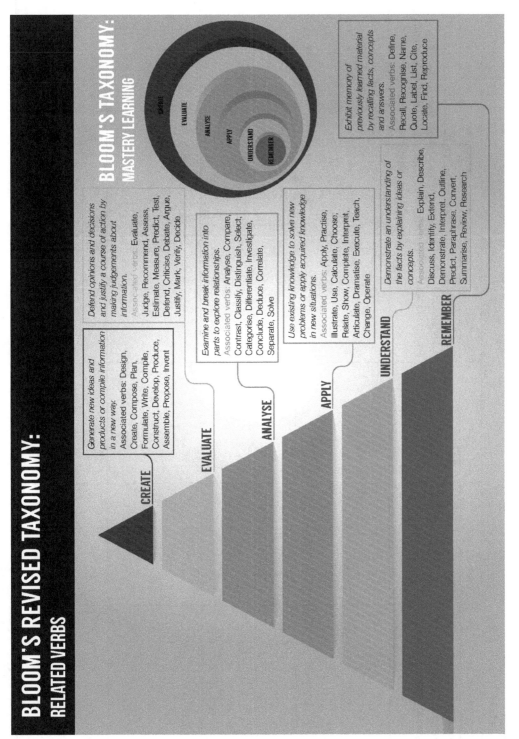

Figure 6.1 Bloom's Revised Taxonomy. Created by GetSmarter, a subsidiary of 2U, Inc., and used with permission.[1]

Table 6.1

Learning Goal	Bloom's Level	Verb	Details	Learning Objective
Understand the key differences among psychodynamic theories	Analyze	Differentiate	Psychoanalysis, Adlerian, and Psychosocial	Students will be able to ***differentiate*** between the primary psychodynamic theories of psychoanalysis, Adlerian therapy, and psychosocial development

Once you have this information you can begin to put it together and develop learning objectives. To give yourself some practice imagine that you are teaching a master's-level counseling theories course. Consider what your learning goals are for the course and for individual assignments. Use the template in Table 6.1 and the initial example to guide you.

Examples of Effective and Ineffective Learning Objectives

Kristi Cannon

Learning objectives can be written at the course level and the individual assignment level. Course-level learning objectives are those learning goals you expect students to achieve at the end of a course. They are broader, to encompass integrated learning, and reflect the summative goals of the course. In contrast, assignment learning objectives are those that reflect specific learning goals for individual assignments and are considered more formative. Assignment learning objectives are focused on smaller pockets of learning and are more specific than those written for the course.

Regardless of the level of objective, there are important considerations to keep in mind when writing learning objectives in order to make them effective.

- **Measurable**. Learning objectives must be built using verbs that are measurable, otherwise we are unable to assess them. Avoid verbs such as know, understand, accept, believe, think, and value, which we cannot directly measure.
- **Single verb**. Each learning objective must be tied to a single action verb. Placing multiple verbs in the learning objective prevents us from knowing which to assess or how to assess them both.
- **Clear**. Learning objectives should clearly outline what the learning goal is and how it will be demonstrated.
- **Concise**. Learning objectives should be written so that they succinctly cover the specific learning goal. Learning objectives written for a course should be broad enough to encompass multiple assignments that demonstrate learning in that area, whereas individual assignment objectives should contain a greater level of specificity. In either case, the learning objective should be concise and cover only the necessary information.
- **Alignment**. Learning objectives written at the assignment level should be aligned to course level objectives based on content and level. They should

be equal to or less than the highest level of cognitive skill required by a course objective. This is because course objectives are broad, meant to encompass multiple assignment objectives, and reflect the highest level of learning expected in the course for that area.

Let's consider a couple of examples from a crisis intervention course. Using the criteria above, select the most effective learning objective from the categories below. Refer to the analysis section below to confirm your findings.

Course Learning Objectives

1. Compile appropriate resources to support clients experiencing symptoms of trauma
2. Analyze and understand trauma-informed treatment approaches and interventions for a variety of crisis situations to support counseling sessions
3. Create a self-care plan to support personal well-being when working with trauma-impacted clients

Assignment Learning Objectives

1. Review and evaluate resources for use in counseling victims of crisis
2. Identify an empirically-validated treatment intervention appropriate for working with children in a crisis situation
3. Summarize sufficient research studies to support adolescent suicide prevention through direct intervention

Analysis

Course Learning Objectives

The most effective learning outcome in this category is option #1. It meets all of the outlined criteria.

There are several concerns with the second option. First, it contains multiple verbs and one of those is not measurable (understand). In addition, it is verbose—consisting of multiple verbs and nouns with far too much context for a course-level objective. That being said, when looking at it in terms of alignment to the learning objectives, we see that there is clear alignment between the objectives and the course objective is the higher-order objective.

The third option has many strengths. It is clear, concise, and demonstrates the use of a single, measurable verb. However, unlike the two options before it, there is no alignment to the assignment learning objectives. Assuming these were to be linked, there is no direct connection between self-care and client resources/interventions.

Assignment Learning Objectives

The most effective learning outcome in this category is option #2. It meets all of the outlined criteria.

The first option has a couple of challenges. First, it includes two verbs. Second, while clear, concise and aligned to the course learning objective, it is fairly broad and may not be quite specific enough for an assignment level objective.

The third option uses only a single verb and demonstrates more specificity than the first. It also maintains good alignment to the course learning objective. However, the drawback with this learning objective is that it is vague and struggles with measurability—how does the student know what is sufficient?

Connecting Learning Objectives to Learning Outcomes

Kristi Cannon

In the last activity you learned about the connection between course level objectives and assignment level objectives. Namely, course objectives are broader and intended to encompass the overall learning goals of the course. They are typically limited to between four and six objectives for the entire course. On the other hand, assignment learning objectives are more specific. They are tied to the direct assignment or learning activity of a set period of time and are intended to function at or below the learning level of the course outcome. One other key differentiator between assignment objectives and course objectives is that course objectives are not directly assessed. Instead, we assess at the assignment level and use the combination of multiple assignment assessment to demonstrate overall mastery of the course learning objective. To that end, every assignment level objective should be aligned to a course level objective. Further, if students are successfully achieving all of the learning objectives at the assignment level, we can deduce that they have mastered the course learning objectives.

In addition to the need for alignment between assignment level objectives and course level objectives, there is also the need to align your course objectives to the program level. Program level learning goals are frequently referred to as learning outcomes or program learning outcomes. Much like course objectives are written to establish the broad goals of the course, program learning outcomes are established by educational programs to outline the overall learning goals of the program. As you might expect, these are broadly written and intended to be demonstrated through the work completed in multiple courses within the program. Alignment between program learning outcomes and course objectives is nearly identical to the process for aligning assignment objectives to course objectives, except the focus is on the course. That is, we align course objectives to the broader program outcomes. And much like we would expect to have multiple assignments aligned to a course objective, we expect that there will be multiple courses in a program of study that would align to the broader program outcomes, based on the course objectives.

Alignment between objectives and outcomes is of great value. It demonstrates a strong link to the goals set forth by a program and ensures that there are effective ways to assess for learning. Proper alignment also means that students graduating from a program are actually meeting the learning outcomes set by the program. As you might imagine, that is pretty important! To that end, the alignment process should always start at the program outcome level and work its way down. By the time you are developing outcomes for a course, the course itself has likely been aligned to the program outcomes already. However, it is important to keep this in mind and ensure you are building your course to meet any program outcomes aligned to it. In the same vein, individual assignment objectives should be built from the course objectives. These are considered the key goals of the course, so all assignments should lead back to these. Working backward and with the main learning goals in mind, will ensure you are always properly aligned and demonstrating good assessment practices that ensure the learning success of your students.

Below is a visual cross-walk of the alignment from a single program outcome to course objectives in courses that would likely be tied to that program outcome. Taking the initial example from the crisis and trauma course, and utilizing the knowledge from your previous activities, try to develop one course objective and at least two assignment objectives that would align the counseling practicum course to the larger program outcome. Remember to begin with the course objective and build down.

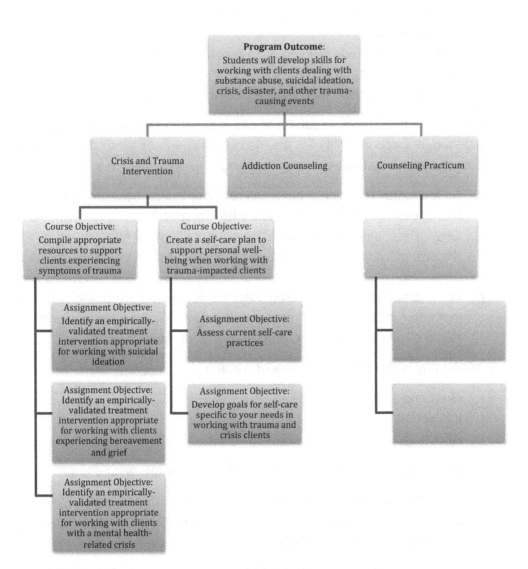

Figure 6.2

Quiz

1. Which characteristic best describes teacher-centered instruction?

   a. Teaching dominated by the instructor through lectures and teacher-led discussions

   b. Instruction that is dominated by the professor and students for optimal learning

   c. Teaching is implemented by a sole authority in the classroom

2. Student-centered learning can be helpful in engaging students and promoting student accountability for their learning. Which of these descriptions best describes student-centered learning?

   a. An instructor teaching a multicultural class brings counseling experts to discuss counseling individuals with disabilities

   b. One of the assignments in a multicultural counseling course is to discuss a current event and lead a discussion on privilege and oppression

   c. An example of a counseling session is viewed in class and the instructor processes with students how effective the session was in terms of promoting a safe, empathic environment

3. Andragogy is the art and science of helping _____ learn.

   a. Graduate students

   b. Individuals

   c. Adults

4. Assumptions of adult learners consist of all of the following except

   a. Self-directed learning becomes more apparent due to maturity

   b. Experience is integral in learning and accommodating new information

   c. Learning needs to be engaging and fun

5. Which description best explains kinesthetic learners in a counseling skills course?

   a. Students are paired in triad groups where one student is the counselor, client, and observer. The students role play a counseling session for 10 minutes

   b. Students view a counseling video and provide feedback on the skills the counselor used in session

c. Students are organized in fishbowl (inner circle of students and outer circle of observers) and discuss how they used reflection of feeling in session

6. A learning contract, by definition is

a. A contract between students and instructors that detail expectations, requirements, and evaluation of student learning
b. A legal contract between students and instructors
c. A verbal agreement between students with disabilities and instructor for accommodations

7. The revised version of Bloom's Taxonomy consists of: remembering, understanding, applying, analyzing, evaluating, and creating. Which scenario best describes the domain of *evaluating*?

a. Students in a counseling practicum class provide feedback to their peers' counseling sessions
b. Students discuss a client case through the perspectives of Adlerian and Cognitive Behavioral theories
c. Students develop their own personal theory of counseling at the end of practicum

8. Kolb (1984) conceptualized different learning styles. Which learning style is associated with "hands-on" activities and learning by actively engaging in a task?

a. Converger
b. Diverger
c. Accommodator

9. Counseling research has reported that experiential learning benefits which of the following?

a. Cultural competence
b. Professional development
c. Both A and B

10. One of the first steps when creating a new course is

a. Creation of learning objectives
b. Choose course activities
c. Design exam questions

11. Which of the following is NOT a characteristic of an effective learning objective?

   a. Measurable
   b. Unattainable
   c. Relevant

12. Course learning objectives should be generated from the following sources except

   a. The instructor's scholarly interests
   b. Professional counseling competencies
   c. Fortune cookie messages

13. According to Van Melle and Pinchin's (2008) A-B-C-D model of learning objectives, C represents

   a. The course for which learning objectives are created
   b. The conditions in which learning objectives will be met
   c. The level of concreteness of learning objectives

14. According to Cabaniss (2008), learning objectives for clinical courses can be classified into the following categories except

   a. Assessment and diagnosis
   b. Empathy development
   c. Self-care strategies

15. When using Bloom's Taxonomy for constructing learning objectives, it is crucial to make sure that verbs used for individual lesson objectives at a low enough taxonomy level to support overall course objectives.

   a. True
   b. False

Note

1 GetSmarter. (n.d.). Bloom's revised taxonomy. Retrieved from www.getsmarter.com/career-advice/win/unpacking-blooms-taxonomy-part-1.

7 Curriculum Development

Designing a course to meet course objectives and student learning outcomes takes practice and creativity as well as attention to best practices in counselor education. This chapter will offer a sample syllabus and applied exercises designed to promote skill growth in course development including how to build a course, deliver the course, and create effective learning outcomes to assess student performance.

- Sample syllabus
- Guided questions to assist in creating a syllabus
- Example course development
- Exercise in writing a lesson plan
- Quiz

Sample Syllabus

J. Kelly Coker

Quarter: Winter
Year: 2017–18
Course Section/Number: COUN 600 02
Course Title: Counseling Theory
Course Units: 3
Date & Time: Wednesdays 6:00 to 7:30 PM PST

Instructor Name: Dr. XXX
Instructor Contact: (put e-mail and business number here)
Office hours: Mondays, 11:00 to 2:00 and by appointment

Course Description

> It is important in your course description to be sure this information matches the course description in the course catalog.

This course will provide an introduction to counseling theories that will lead to an understanding and applied knowledge of theoretical treatment approaches. The focus is on the application and integration of counseling theories in clinical mental health counseling practice.

Course Prerequisites & Assumptions

> I always include prerequisites and assumptions in my syllabi. This statement works for both in-person and on-line classes, and sets expectations for professional dispositions and behavior.

There are no prerequisites for this course, but I do have some assumptions about our time together this quarter. Counseling department students are expected to conduct themselves with professionalism at all times. Appropriate professional etiquette is expected in all communications with other classmates, instructors and practicum site personnel.

Professionalism and classroom etiquette requires student attentiveness and engagement. It is unprofessional to utilize computers, tablets and smartphones in class for purposes that are not directly related to the current class topic and presentation. Residential course instructors have the option to make their classrooms "computer, tablet and smartphone free" and are authorized to take away participation and professionalism points for unauthorized technology use during class. When residential students ask to take notes in class with their computer, tablet and smartphone the faculty can request the student verify notes were taken and the technology was used as agreed. Distance learning students should abide by the same principles as they self-regulate their own professional conduct during Zoom Meeting course discussions. If you wouldn't do it in a residential classroom, then don't do it in a virtual one!

Behavior and written or verbal exchanges that are disrespectful, harassing, or otherwise professionally inappropriate are not acceptable of counseling professionals. Students engaging in these behaviors will be counseled immediately. Students need to treat classroom engagements in a similar manner as they would engage with colleagues in a professional agency/counseling environment. Incidents of unprofessional conduct will be referred to the program director and your advisor and noted on the student's advising record. Repeated offenses will result in referral to the Student Evaluation Committee to determine the appropriateness of the student's continuation in the program.

Self-Reflection and Disclosure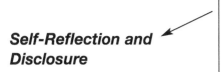

In counseling programs, it can be helpful to have an agreed-upon statement regarding disclosure. Counseling courses often lend themselves to personal reflection and disclosure, and it is important to share this information and clarify the implications.

The Master's of Counseling Program is committed to student education, safety, and integrity of well-prepared counselors and therapists. As part of this commitment, all students in the Counseling Program are expected to engage in personal growth and self-discovery. As a means to personal growth, self-discovery, and awareness, students are often asked to reflect on personal experiences and reactions (past and present) and share these experiences in classroom settings (i.e., engage in self-disclosure). While we do not engage in counseling or psychotherapy in the context of the Counseling Program, areas of growth are often identified during these self-disclosure processes. Your course grade is not contingent on what you share or the extent of your self-disclosure. The implications of your self-disclosure, however, may include reporting information to other faculty, program remediation, program dismissal, ethic charges, requirement to attend counseling, and/or notification to authorities. For additional information on self-disclosure, please refer to the ACA Code of Ethics, Section F.7.b. Student Welfare.

Method(s) of Instruction

> Sharing in the syllabus what to expect from the professor is essential. How will you teach the course? What are students expected to do? How will the course be delivered? This particular course has both asynchronous and synchronous components.

* The primary method of instruction for this course is based upon a series of independent readings, case studies, class discussions, and weekly lectures.
* Critical Questions are posed and answered in asynchronous Canvas discussions using the assigned readings as key references.
* Students will participate in live (synchronous) course discussions for 1.5 hours each week. Wednesdays, 6:00–7:30 PM PACIFIC Time Zone
* Students will take 3 quizzes covering content from the text and other readings.
* Students will create and present a professional presentation describing their current theoretical orientation as applied to a particular setting and client.

Credit Hour Requirements

3 Credits earned over 11 Week Quarter

Required Reading(s)

Sommers-Flanagan, J. & Sommers-Flanagan, R. (2015). Counseling and Psychotherapy Theories in Context and Practice, with Video Resource Center: Skills, Strategies, and Techniques, 2nd ed. Hoboken, NJ: John Wiley & Sons, Inc. ISBN-10: 1119084202/ISBN-13: 978–1119084204. [EISBN-10: 111908 7899/EISBN-13: 9781119087892].

For other required readings, please see the resources for each week in the Modules area of Canvas.

Recommended readings

Frankl, V. (1959). Man's Search for Meaning. New York, NY: Washington Square Press.

Required Software

Please see all technology requirements in the Modules area of your Canvas classroom.

Program Learning Outcomes

The table below shows the MA in Counseling Program and Student Learning Outcomes as they align with the University Institutional Learning Goals

Many universities expect that syllabi include information about program learning outcomes, institutional outcomes, and course outcomes. It is important to know the expected format for this information and should be consistently included across program syllabi.

MA COUNSELING PROGRAM GOALS AND STUDENT LEARNING OUTCOMES version 15 September 2017	INSTITUTIONAL LEARNING GOALS							
	1	2	3	4	5	6	7	8
	Disciplinary Knowledge and Skill	Critical Thinking	Scientific and Quantitative Reasoning	Cultural Competence in a Diverse World	Communication	Literacy	Moral and Ethical Responsibility	Community Engagement and Service
OUTCOME 1— Assessment and research acumen. Graduates will acquire, refine, and demonstrate appropriate Master's level ability to assess client issues and to incorporate evidence-based counseling practices in a variety of settings.	x	x	x			x		

MA COUNSELING PROGRAM GOALS AND STUDENT LEARNING OUTCOMES version 15 September 2017	INSTITUTIONAL LEARNING GOALS							
	1	2	3	4	5	6	7	8
	Disciplinary Knowledge and Skill	Critical Thinking	Scientific and Quantitative Reasoning	Cultural Competence in a Diverse World	Communication	Literacy	Moral and Ethical Responsibility	Community Engagement and Service
OUTCOME 2— Professional identity. Graduates will develop a professional identity as a counselor as well as the dispositions related to effective practice, including integrity, sensitivity, flexibility, insight, compassion, and personal presence.	X				X		X	
OUTCOME 3— Leadership. Graduates will become an organizational leader, a group process expert, and a positive force in achieving high levels of participation, cooperation and cohesion.					X			X
OUTCOME 4— Social justice. Graduates will develop an understanding of various cultures and the implications of diversity for social justice. They will				X			X	X

MA COUNSELING PROGRAM GOALS AND STUDENT LEARNING OUTCOMES version 15 September 2017	INSTITUTIONAL LEARNING GOALS							
	1	2	3	4	5	6	7	8
	Disciplinary Knowledge and Skill	Critical Thinking	Scientific and Quantitative Reasoning	Cultural Competence in a Diverse World	Communication	Literacy	Moral and Ethical Responsibility	Community Engagement and Service
demonstrate insight into the social and psychological implications of socioeconomic position and how poverty and social stress can affect an individual's mental health and recovery.				X			X	X
OUTCOME 5— Wellness and resilience orientation. Graduates will incorporate the principles of optimal career and lifespan development towards promoting a resilience and wellness across the lifespan.								X
OUTCOME 6— Ethical Compliance and risk management. Graduates will learn to manage the risks of a professional counseling practice, ensure personal and client safety, and remain compliant with all laws and regulations and moral and ethical guidelines.							X	

MA COUNSELING PROGRAM GOALS AND STUDENT LEARNING OUTCOMES version 15 September 2017	INSTITUTIONAL LEARNING GOALS							
	1	2	3	4	5	6	7	8
	Disciplinary Knowledge and Skill	Critical Thinking	Scientific and Quantitative Reasoning	Cultural Competence in a Diverse World	Communication	Literacy	Moral and Ethical Responsibility	Community Engagement and Service
OUTCOME 7— Systemic practice. Graduates will integrate a systems approach to conceptualizing client development, presenting issues, and counseling strategies and approaches.	x			x		x		
OUTCOME 8— Credentialing and Licensure. Graduates will demonstrate knowledge of how to become a licensed Professional Clinical Counselor or Marriage or Family Counselor in California or achieve a similar license in the other states and territories of the United States, Canada and other international partners.	x							x

MA COUNSELING PROGRAM GOALS AND STUDENT LEARNING OUTCOMES version 15 September 2017	INSTITUTIONAL LEARNING GOALS							
	1	2	3	4	5	6	7	8
	Disciplinary Knowledge and Skill	Critical Thinking	Scientific and Quantitative Reasoning	Cultural Competence in a Diverse World	Communication	Literacy	Moral and Ethical Responsibility	Community Engagement and Service
OUTCOME 9 (MCFC Track Only)—Professional Practice. Graduates will acquire, refine, and demonstrate appropriate knowledge, skills, and dispositions to effectively work with couples, families, and other systems in a variety of settings.	X	X			X			X
OUTCOME 10 (CMHC Track Only)—Professional Practice. Graduates will acquire, refine, and demonstrate appropriate knowledge, skills, and dispositions to effectively assess, diagnose, and treat clients in a variety of settings.	X	X			X			X

Course Learning Outcomes

Course outcomes for this course are based on the 2016 Council for the Accreditation of and Related Educational Programs (CACREP) Standards.

In CACREP programs, including a table to show which standards are covered in the course and the associated learning activities is helpful to include. This information should be consistent across all sections of the same course.

	Learning Outcomes At the completion of this course:	CACREP Common Core Curricular Areas	CACREP CMHC Specialty	CACREP MCFC Specialty	Related Assignments, Readings, and Lectures
1	Student identifies and analyzes theories and models of counseling.	2.F.5.a	5.C.1.b	5.F.1.b	Weeks 2–9: Readings, discussion posts, lectures. Weeks 5, 8 and 10: Quiz
2	Student identifies and integrates a systems approach to conceptualizing clients.	2.F.5.b		5.F.1.a	Week 9: Readings, discussion post, lecture. Week 10: Quiz
3	Student identifies and integrates evidence-based counseling strategies and techniques for prevention and intervention.	2.F.5.j	5.C.3.b		Week 10: Final Project-Counseling Theories

Grading

Performance Evaluation Criteria:
Your final grade for this course will come from four primary areas: Weekly activities and discussion posts and responses, weekly participation in scheduled classes, three scheduled quizzes, and a prepared presentation identifying your theoretical orientation. Please see a more detailed description of each element below:

> Clearly identifying how students are evaluated over the course of the term provides clarity about where their final grade comes from. Setting expectations in the syllabus and again in the classroom (if online) or regularly throughout the term in person (if on-ground) ensures students understand what is expected of them.

1) Discussion Posts: Most weeks, there will be a discussion prompt related to the readings and outside class activities and other provided materials for the week. You can earn up to 5 points for each discussion. Please see the discussion rubric for details. Discussion posts are worth 40% of your final course grade.
2) Weekly Class Meetings: Each week we will meet via Zoom for an hour and a half class discussion. Please attend each session and be prepared to actively participate and engage. A lack of presence (including a lack of video presence), participation, or engagement can result in a deduction of points from your final grade. Participation is worth 10% of your final course grade.
3) Quizzes: This course contains three quizzes covering content from the text and other readings. The multiple choice exams are intended to help prepare students for the National Counselor Exam (NCE), which is required by many states for licensure. Quizzes are worth 30% of your final grade.
4) Theory Presentation: You will develop a presentation using power point or other presentation software identifying the theoretical orientation you most identify with at this point in your training. The presentation is worth 20% of your final grade. Your presentation should contain the following components:

   a) The setting and population with which you intend to work.
   b) One or two (but no more than two) theoretical orientations you plan to use in your work. Be sure to include the basic tenets of the theory, empirical support for its use with your anticipated population, and the reason this theory is the best fit for your anticipated work.

c) Examples of processes or techniques (at least two per theory presented) that you will use in your clinical work. Please describe (or even demonstrate) the technique as well as the rationale for its use.

d) Appropriate citations throughout and a reference slide or slides at the end identifying your sources. NOTE: sources should be primary sources including textbook, textbook chapters, refereed journal articles. Try to avoid webpages as source material.

Once you finish your power point presentation, you will record yourself presenting the information via Zoom. Your presentation should be between 10 and 15 minutes long.

Late Assignments

Expectations about late assignments, participation, attendance, and incompletes may be based in university or department policies or may be up to the professor's discretion. In either case, providing this information can help get in front of these issues with students should they occur.

Assignments that are submitted late without prior arrangement with the professor will be marked down one letter grade for each day that it is late. Please contact the professor ahead of time if you need to request specific accommodations.

Incompletes

Incompletes are, as a general rule, not given. However, in extreme (and well-documented) circumstances they may be assigned. Incomplete grades for students holding less than a "B-" average will not be considered. If you are having personal issues that are inferring with your ability to work on the course (and we all do from time to time), you will need to contact me before things get out of control. If you wait until the end of the course to tell me you've been struggling, it will be unfair to your classmates if we renegotiate our class contract.

Further clarification on how grades are computed can be displayed in a table. In addition, showing the university or department breakdown of what constitutes an "A", "B", etc. can be useful.

Graded work	Percentage of final grade
DISCUSSION	40%
PARTICIPATION	10%
QUIZZES	30%
THEORETICAL PRESENTATION	20%

98–100 = A+
93–97 = A
90–92 = A–
87–89 = B+
83–86 = B
80–82 = B–

Grading Rubric

There is one general rubric for all discussion questions and a rubric for the final project that can be found in the "Assignments" area of your Canvas classroom.

At my institution, the syllabus links to rubrics used as well as institutional policies. It is important that the syllabus includes or at least points to this information.

Institutional Policies

Academic Integrity & Plagiarism
Americans with Disabilities Act (ADA)
Attendance Policy
Classroom and Online Etiquette
Credit Hour Policy
Diversity
Grade Appeals
PAU Email Communication Policy
Syllabus Policy
Video Recording

** Policies can be found in Section 3 of the PAU Catalog or on the Institutional Policies Webpage at www.paloaltou.edu/institutional-policies

Guided Questions to Assist in Creating a Syllabus

Eric T. Beeson

Creating syllabi can be an obligatory practice, the application of a boiler plate across a program, and/or a creative process that begins the student–educator relationship and journey of discovery. Amidst requirement from accreditation bodies and institutions, it can sometimes be challenging to create a syllabus that is in fact a teaching tool. Syllabi are especially important in counselor education because they provide evidence of the knowledge and skills obtained that will be used in licensure applications for years to come. Below are several questions to ask yourself when creating a new syllabus or evaluating those that already exist.

What is Required?

The first step is to decide what information is required in your syllabus by the 2016 CACREP Standards (CACREP, 2015), your college/university, and any other accreditation bodies that your program might be accountable to.

Please review Section 2.D. of the 2016 CACREP Standards and list what elements are required in each syllabus.

_____

_____

Take a look at your college and university policies regarding syllabi and list any additional elements that might be required.

_____

_____

If your program is accredited by another body, then please review their standards and list them below.

_____

_____

Lastly, consult with your state statutes and regulations related to counseling and ensure that your syllabi covered the necessary content and skills necessary for state licensure.

_____

_____

What is Important to Students?

With the required sections in mind, think about what is important to students. Think about the parts of your syllabi that you used when you were a student. Ask the students you work with what they think are the most important parts of the syllabus. As students what they would like to see in a syllabus.

What is Important to You?

In many ways, the syllabus becomes an instructional strategy and an extension of your teaching philosophy. Thinking back to the chapter on teaching philosophy, does your syllabus embody the values that you espoused? This is probably the hardest question for me to answer. For instance, if I align with a feminist perspective, then can I really impose standards and values on another through the syllabus? How do I balance the accountability requirements with my philosophical stance?

_____

_____

What are Some Other Possible Sections?

There are some other sections that many educators have found useful to include in their syllabi. For instance, is it helpful to have a statement about confidentiality in the syllabus? What about student supports? Is it helpful to have contact information for the university counseling services or Title IX office? When thinking about your syllabi, what unique sections do you think would prove useful student success?

_____

_____

Example Course Development

Eric T. Beeson

Designing a PBL Course

Scenario:

You did such a wonderful job incorporating PBL into your class sessions that your department chair would like you to pilot an entire course grounded in PBL learning principles.

As you read this scenario, what do you experience? What goes through your mind? What do you feel? What do you already know? What do you need to know? What are the consequences if you don't successfully navigate this scenario? Where will you find the needed information?

This activity is designed to help you design a problem-based scenario that can be used as a meta-problem that structures the entire course.

- What are your knowledge and/or skill learning outcomes for the course? Think about the CACREP content areas that are addressed as well as what learning outcomes are expected.
- How does a professional counselor encounter the need for this knowledge and skill in the real world?
- What are some real-world problems that require someone to know this content and perform these skills?
- How can you construct a meta-problem scenario that incorporates as many of the real-world scenarios above? Take a moment to write out a scenario that provides the impetus for students to explore the necessary content and demonstrate the necessary skills and practices.
- Brainstorm a list of potential assignments and represent sub-problems within the larger meta-problem designed for this course.
- For both the meta- and sub-problem scenarios above, evaluate the problem scenarios based upon the following characteristics:

  - Is it ill-structured, complex, & authentic?
  - Does it activate students' prior learning and situational interest?
  - Is there more than one potential answer?
  - Does it contain sub-cues to stimulate discussion and encourage students to search for explanations?

- Does it encourage and engage diverse learners in self-directed learning?
- Is it tailored to students' stage of development and cognitive complexity?
- Does it occur frequently in the real world?
- Are there real consequences if this situation is handled poorly?
- Is the scenario familiar or unfamiliar?

• Think about how your individual course sessions will also fit into both the meta- and sub-problem scenarios. How can you design your "lectures" using PBL principles?

• Review the following examples that were used in an Assessment in Counseling course.

PBL-Course Description

This course is built on the principles of problem-based learning (PBL). PBL is a method of instruction that uses real-world scenarios as the organizing structure of course content. Scenarios are designed to guide students to the necessary content areas and learning outcomes. Students use their resources (e.g., textbook) to guide a self-directed process of discovery.

This course is organized in a way that assumes the students have been hired by one of the premier behavioral health care agencies in the United States, Enriched Counseling & Wellness Services, Inc. (ECWS, Inc.). During their first day, they learn that ECWS, Inc. recently had a reaccreditation site visit by the Accreditation Commission for Health Care. After the site visit, ECWS, Inc. was placed on a two-year probationary period due to an inability to provide evidence for their use of appropriate assessment strategies, especially those related to therapeutic outcomes. During this two-year period, ECWS, Inc. must strengthen its use of assessment strategies, or the agency will lose its accreditation and be forced to close. As a result, ECWS, Inc. has hired many new staff (students in this course) to ensure their accreditation continues.

In essence, students are not just enrolled in a course but hired by an agency that needs their skills and expertise to continue providing quality services. Therefore, most of the activities in this course will take place in this hypothetical agency and mimic real-world practice. These hypothetical scenarios are not reflective of any actual students, clients, or situations, and any similarities are merely coincidence.

PBL Assignments

Assignment #1: Unit Quizzes

Description:

ECWS, Inc. has prepared a comprehensive staff orientation program that is designed to ensure you have the minimum knowledge and skills to excel in the agency. Additionally, this orientation program is structured to help new counselors prepare for the National Counselor Exam. Therefore, each unit of this course includes quizzes that will serve as formative assessment to ensure minimum knowledge comprehension. Quizzes are untimed and may be taken up to three times. At least one attempt is required at least 24 hours before our weekly "staff meeting" (a.k.a., the live session). Each unit quiz will cover all asynchronous and synchronous material in each unit. Quiz format may include multiple choice, true/false, short answer, and fill-in-the-blank.

Assignment #2: Become an Expert Project—Assessment Strategy Critique

Description:

Given the diverse client population at ECWS, Inc., it is important for the counselors to be familiar with a wide range of assessment strategies. During your last staff meeting at ECWS, Inc., your clinical supervisor asked you to become an expert on an assessment strategy of your choice. You are asked to select a specific assessment strategy (e.g., Quality of Life Inventory, Adult Attachment Interview) and evaluate its characteristics (e.g., length, cost, psychometric properties, etc.). Then, you will prepare a report and present your findings at a future "staff meeting."

Assignment #3: Unstructured Clinical Interview Report

Description:

Your supervisor at ECWS, Inc. believes the current intake process is faulty and asks you to revise it. Therefore, you are asked to create an unstructured clinical interview template that can be used by all ECWS, Inc. employees. Your supervisor also believes it is important for counselors to personally complete any assessment that they will use with clients. She believes this promotes self-reflection and understanding of the client experience during the assessment process. Therefore, she would like you to complete a report using your unstructured clinical interview template as if you are your own client.

- What do you think about the examples that have been provided?

Exercise in Writing a Lesson Plan

Eric T. Beeson

Scenario:

After attending a recent training by the Center for Innovative Teaching at your university, your department chair returns charging you to infuse problem-based learning principles in your next live class session.

As you read this scenario, what do you experience? What goes through your mind? What do you feel? What do you already know? What do you need to know? What are the consequences if you don't successfully navigate this scenario? Where will you find the needed information?

This activity is designed to help you design a problem-based scenario that can be used in a single class session.

- What are your knowledge and/or skill learning outcomes for the class session? Think about the CACREP content areas that are addressed as well as what learning outcomes are expected.
- How does a professional counselor encounter the need for this knowledge and skill in the real world?
- What are some real-world problems that require someone to know this content and perform these skills?
- How can you construct a problem scenario that mimics the real-world scenario above? Take a moment to write out a scenario that provides the impetus for students to explore the necessary content and demonstrate the necessary skills and practices.
- Evaluate the problem scenarios based upon the following characteristics:

    - Is it ill-structured, complex, & authentic?
    - Does it activate students' prior learning and situational interest?
    - Is there more than one potential answer?

- Does it contain sub-cues to stimulate discussion and encourage students to search for explanations?
- Does it encourage and engage diverse learners in self-directed learning?
- Is it tailored to students' stage of development and cognitive complexity?
- Does it occur frequently in the real world?
- Are there real consequences if this situation is handled poorly?
- Is the scenario familiar or unfamiliar?

- Revise your problem scenario as necessary to incorporate as many of these characteristics as necessary.
- Next, take your existing PowerPoint, lecture, etc. and place this scenario at the beginning. This might sound backwards. Traditionally, the content comes first and then the case example is provided to apply. With PBL, this order is reversed; the problem scenario comes first as the driving force towards student learning outcomes. Both anecdotally as well as in the empirical literature, the presentation of the problem first increases interest, activates existing knowledge, and identifies gaps that students are more eager to fill because the content that will follow now has relevance. When I back-fill with content, I typically find that anything I would have said in a lecture has already been uncovered through the social discovery process of working through the problem scenario in both small and large groups. For any information that hasn't been covered, this backfilling process ensures that all content has been covered and learning outcomes demonstrated.

Quiz

1. Why is it important to incorporate and identify CACREP 2016 core and specialty standards in the development of curriculum?

   a. These standards provide some good ideas about what could be included in a course.
   b. These standards represent the accrediting body's expectations for what must be taught to counseling professionals in CACREP accredited programs.
   c. All counseling programs are required to include these standards in their course syllabi.

    d. These standards often frame student learning outcomes for particular curricular areas.

    e. Both a & c.

    f. Both b & d.

2. When asked to develop a course previously taught by someone else in your program, it is generally acceptable to:

    a. Just use exactly what was taught before; fundamental content does not tend to change.

    b. Change every aspect of the course from how it was taught before; it is important to make is solely your own.

    c. Use a blend of both previously-taught content and newer content derived from more recent research and best practice in the field of study you are teaching.

    d. Be sure to include everything you can find on the topic you are teaching; learners need to be exposed to it all.

3. Learning objectives represent:

    a. The building blocks of the course content.

    b. The CACREP standards you need to meet in the course.

    c. The student learning outcomes (SLOs) learners will be expected to demonstrate.

    d. Bloom's Taxonomy

4. According to Zaghab and Beckenholdt (2014), what should be considered when determining whether to use a textbook or not?

    a. Is the field of study in a state of dynamism and change?

    b. Is the class likely to be boring or interesting?

    c. Is the information in a state of enduring equilibrium?

    d. Both a and b.

    e. Both b and c.

    f. Both a and c.

5. In selecting other learning materials for a course, it is important to:

    a. Only pick materials that represent one style of learning; you don't want to be confusing.

    b. Focus primarily on materials that support a "read/lecture/test" format.

   c. Focus primarily on materials that support a "read/debate/view/practice/demonstrate" format.
   d. Use only digital products and no paper products.

6. Universal Design (UD) principles:

   a. Are used to incorporate flexible options in curriculum development.
   b. Take into account learner variability.
   c. Solely used in the field of architecture.
   d. Both a and b.
   e. None of the above.

7. In developing a course for online delivery, it is important to:

   a. Only use what you would also use in a face-to-face version of the class.
   b. Build the course so students have to read more than they would in a face-to-face version.
   c. Consider how to use a variety of learning materials including readings, media, and interactive modules.
   d. Both a and b.

8. According to Hrastinski (2008):

   a. Online learners benefit from a blend of synchronous and asynchronous activities.
   b. Online learners are most successful when courses contain only asynchronous activities.
   c. Online learners are most successful when courses contain only synchronous activities.
   d. Neither work well for online learning.

9. The syllabus is used to communicate

   a. To all stakeholders what student should learn as a result of completing the course experience.
   b. To students a clear understanding of the learning expectations throughout the course.
   c. To students the learning outcomes as a result of the educational experience.
   d. To students the tenor of the course.
   e. All of the above.

10. The syllabus

    a. Is one strategy for relationship building between the professor and students.
    b. Is the only strategy for relationship building between the professor and students.
    c. Is an opportunity to guide learners with clear expectations.
    d. Can be used to help students understand how a course contributes to his or her professional preparation.
    e. All except b.

11. Andragogy is

    a. Synonymous with pedagogy.
    b. The science of teaching adults.
    c. The science of teaching on-line.
    d. The science of teaching and learning.

12. According to Cicco (2012), counseling courses

    a. Should include assignments that allow student to practice their counseling skills throughout the program.
    b. Should never be taught on-line.
    c. Should allow student the opportunity to prepare for credentialing examinations.
    d. Both b and c.
    e. None of the above.

13. As an instructor, you will need to

    a. Be consistent and congruent with course expectations for your students and for yourself.
    b. Be flexible and open to changing the course expectations as the term progresses.
    c. Always be available to respond to students within four hours of their e-mail inquiries.
    d. Communicate clearly to students that you have the authority to make changes to the requirements of the course any time you deem appropriate.

14. One of the differences between on-line course syllabi and syllabi for face to face courses, is

    a. The syllabi for on-line courses do not include as much information as the syllabi for face to face courses.
    b. The syllabi for on-line course should include as many or, in most cases, more details than the syllabi for face to face courses.
    c. The syllabi for on-line courses do not need to include information about accommodations for students with disabilities.
    d. The syllabi for on-line courses do not need to include learning outcomes.

15. Which of the following is *not* a recommended component of the syllabus

    a. Instructor's home address.
    b. Course title.
    c. Course grading scale.
    d. Schedule of activities.
    e. Philosophy of teaching.

References

Cicco, G. (2012). Counseling instruction in the online classroom: A survey of faculty and student perceptions. *i-manager's Journal on School Educational Technology*, 8(2), 1–10.

Hrastinski, S. (2008). Asynchronous and Synchronous E-Learning. *Educause Quarterly*, 4, 51–55.

Zaghab, R. W., & Beckenholdt, P. (2014). *Textbook-free learning: A framework for critical analysis*. Paper presented at the International Conference on eLearning. 190–199. Retrieved from http://search.proquest.com.ezp.waldenulibrary.org/doc view/1545530948?accountid=14872.

8 Evaluation of Student Learning

Instructor Feedback and Developmental Assessment

Learning how to assess students' counseling skills, knowledge, and professional development is a skill new counselor educators must develop. There are a variety of ways to do so within each course and across the counseling program. This chapter will provide supplemental materials to assist building insight and promoting skill development in formative and summative assessment including how to build assessment instruments and deliver feedback. It will include:

- Example formative and summative assessments (rubric)

- Sample syllabus and questions to develop appropriate assessments

- Samples of feedback (compare and contrast good and bad)

- Quiz

Example Formative and Summative Assessments (Rubric)

Esther Benoit

Family Process and Development Group Read Activity and Rubric

One of the key concepts we are working on in this course is the importance of systemic and developmental changes and their impact on families. Students are introduced to the concept of systemic/relational thinking at the start of the term and are asked to apply systemic case conceptualization regularly throughout the course. As each new construct is shared knowledge checks are completed in the form of short assignments/assessments.

Peer-Presentation of Reading Content (Group Read!)

In the first two weeks of the course, knowledge checks are done through class discussions that focus on the initial readings. Students are asked to focus on one key term or concept (depending on class size they might be asked to do more than one) and bring a short synopsis of that concept to the class discussion to present to their peers. This peer teaching helps make the weekly readings more manageable and creates a sense of shared responsibility in the learning process.

Students are evaluated on their understanding of the construct and their ability to present it succinctly and accurately. A 4-point rubric is used to assess this learning activity.

Sample Syllabus and Questions to Develop Appropriate Assessments

Joy S. Whitman

Once you have developed the learning objectives and outcomes for the course you develop and the kinds of activities in which students will engage, it is time to craft assessments for learning. In this workbook, you are offered ample examples of how you can do so. The rubrics in Table 8.1 provide you with an idea about how to evaluate student performance. The activity that follows this one offers examples of how to offer feedback.

Table 8.1 Group Read Rubric

Comprehension	Concept is explained fully, relevant examples are shared to illustrate concept. 2 points	Concept is explained partially, key elements of concept are not explored or not explored fully. 1 point	Concept is not explained 0 points
Total points: 2			
Presentation/ Teaching	Explanation is clear and concise 1 point	Explanation is unclear or rambles on .5 point	No presentation given 0 points
Total points: 1			
Group Engagement	Engaged in group discussion-asks at least 1 question of peers 1 point	Some group engagement .5 point	No group participation 0 points
Total points: 1			
Total Points Possible: 4			

This activity provides you with an incomplete syllabus and asks you to then develop what you believe are appropriate assessments of student learning. Using the learning objectives, what are some appropriate assessments you can create? One assignment is offered as a start. Are there formative and summative assignments appropriate that can capture the learning objectives? Consider as well for each assignment a rubric that will guide your evaluation. The text offers you an example of a rubric as well as the example in the preceding activity and others throughout this workbook. Have fun!

Sample of Incomplete Syllabus

COUN XXX—Year, Section
Course Name: Introduction to the Counseling Profession

Instructor: XXX
Office: XXX
Office Phone: XXX.XXX.XXXX
Office Hours: XXXX
Email: XXX

Required Texts

Neukrug, E. (2015). *The world of the counselor: An introduction to the counseling profession* (5th ed.). Pacific Grove, CA: Thomson Brooks Cole.

American Psychological Association. (2009). *Publication manual of the American Psychological Association* (6th ed.). Washington, DC: APA.

Required selected readings (at end of syllabus)

Course Instruction

This course will include interactive learning, small group work, writing assignments, class lecture and discussion, and use of Desire to Learn (D2L) technology.

Course Description

This introductory counseling course is designed to provide students with an orientation to the field of counseling. It will familiarize students with the

assumptions, theories, strategies, applications, and ethical and legal considerations related to development in counseling. Students will be introduced
to the core requirements and multicultural competencies necessary to
becoming a counselor, the various employment opportunities and settings
in the counseling profession, and the roles and functions of counselors in
these settings. Central to this course will be an on-going self-evaluation of the
students' attitudes, values, interpersonal skills, and motives for choosing
counseling as a potential profession. Threaded throughout the course will be
the concept of counselor as social change agent and advocate for clients, the
community, and the counseling profession.

Nature of the Hybrid Course

The course is conducted both face-to-face (f2f) and online. That is what
makes it a hybrid course. These various modalities allow you to meet and
build community in person as well as online. The connection between the
various modalities is one of learning collaboration and consultation. The
processes of consultation and collaboration are key to the counseling
professional, as you will soon learn that this profession is one that relies on
the connection with others. Collaborating through group projects and
consulting through the discussion board give you an opportunity to look to
colleagues for assistance and to explore issues with others. We will engage
in the same processes in class and will continue discussions started online in
class.

Course Objectives

After completing this course, students should:

1. Describe the historical, political, social, and philosophical factors that
   have influenced the development of counseling as a profession and how
   contemporary social issues (e.g., technological growth, diversification of
   the population) and present concerns of the profession (e.g., credentialing,
   accreditation, preparation standards) influence the practice of counseling
   in various settings.
2. Develop an awareness of their personal characteristics and beliefs that
   influence their place in the counseling field and their potential role as a
   counselor.

3. Identify roles, functions, work settings, preparation standards, credential-ing, licensure, and professional identity of counselors.
4. Apply the ACA code of ethics and standards of practice, of ethical decision-making processes, and of basic legal guidelines in the field.
5. Identify and scrutinize diversity issues, including worldview, race/ethnicity, gender, social class, spirituality, sexual orientation, age, physical and mental status, and equity issues in counseling.
6. Be able to identify counselor characteristics that influence helping pro-cesses and be able to identify the basic competencies and skills, including consultation and collaboration, necessary to work with diverse populations of clients.
7. Develop advocacy strategies directed toward (a) promoting the profession of counseling, (b) calling attention to institutional barriers that may impede access, equity, and success for clients, and (c) challenging social barriers that impede access, equity, and success for clients.

An Invitation

This course is guided by the assumptions of dignity and respect for all persons in the classroom, which was designed in the hopes of creating a safe and non-threatening environment. Students should feel comfortable speaking with me privately about any concerns related to learning styles and abilities or any other issues that might have an impact on your success in this course. If you know you have or suspect you have a disability for which you may need accommodations, please contact me as soon as possible. In addition, the Center for Students with Disabilities (XXX.XXX.XXXX) is a resource you may wish to consult.

Course Requirements

1. Class Attendance and Participation: All students are expected to complete the assigned readings prior to class discussion. Attendance at all face-to-face class sessions is required. Participation in classroom and online activities, exercises, and discussions is expected, including participation on the discussion board. Each student will contribute his or her fair share and to communicate consistently and professionally with peers and the instructor as part of meeting the requirements for the course.
2. Interview Counseling Professional. Students will interview in person (face-to-face) one counseling professional about the role of professionals and changes and important issues within the field. This professional must

have received her/his training and education as a counselor in a program similar to the Counseling Program. That means she/he must have a degree in counseling, or if she/he is in student affairs, a degree similar to that of counseling or in student affairs. Individuals who received training and education in social work, psychology (anyone who is trained in a counseling psychology program, for example, is not appropriate for this interview), marriage and family therapy, and psychiatry are NOT viable professionals for interviewing even if they are licensed as a LPC or LCPC. If you have any doubt about the training of the individual you plan to interview, please ask her or him about her or his training PRIOR to your interview or contact me to verify that she or he is appropriate for this assignment. Also, you may not interview a family member, employer, or close friend for this assignment. Any deviation from using the appropriate professional will result in a loss of 10 points for the assignment.

If you would like to earn extra credit for this assignment (2 additional points), you have the option to interview another mental health professional. The second professional should be in a different area of counseling or concentration (you may not interview 2 people from the same counseling concentration) or from another helping field such as psychology, social work, psychiatry, marriage and family therapy. You may interview this person only as additional to the one required above.

You are to write a reaction paper to the interview, indicating issues that raised salience for you about the counseling profession, training, the role of the counselor, and current issues within the field. The paper should reflect your awareness of the profession and role as a counselor as opposed to a summary of the interview. I cannot stress enough how important it is not to offer a summary of the interview but your REACTION to it. I am looking for your "inner dialogue" of the interviews. You may discuss the interview but mostly in context of your reaction to the responses. A running account of what was said is not important though it is important to include the items in the Interview Schedule available in this syllabus. This paper should be 8–10 pages in length or 10–12 if interviewing a second mental health professional, excluding the title page.

Now it is your turn to complete the assessments for the course.

- What other assessments might you create and rubrics to guide your evaluation of the assignments?
- How do the assessments connect to the objectives of the course?

Samples of Feedback (Compare and Contrast Good and Bad)

Abby E. Dougherty

Quality feedback is essential to positive learning experiences for both students and educators. Quality feedback can bolster student learning by supporting their strengths, keeping their work goal-directed, and clarify errors. However, giving feedback can be challenging, especially if you are fearful of student's reactions or feel hurried.

One method for providing feedback is called the feedback sandwich. There are three steps to this approach. First, (a) provide positive feedback, (b) provide constructive feedback, (c) close with feedback that will build trust. Additionally, when providing the feedback, ideally the educator links their feedback to the rubric for the assignment. Let's look at an example:

> Tim,
>
> Excellent work analyzing the literature for this week's homework assignment. You were arguments were well supported. In terms of room for improvement, there were several APA errors. For example, you were missing several in-text citations. I want to recommend that you review the learning resources, the assignment rubric, and the feedback I provided directly in your assignment. Many students struggle with APA formatting and I have no doubt your scores will improve with extra attention to learning this material.

Now let's look at a poor example of providing feedback:

> Tim,
>
> Here is your point total:
>
> 25/30

Educators will sometimes provide point totals that do relate back to their rubrics or any other qualitative feedback. Students are left guessing as to why they have had points deducted and what skills are necessary to improve their work. Without some qualitative feedback or a well-developed rubric, students are left guessing about how they can improve their work. Effective feedback is clear, specific, and given regularly.

Another mistake when giving feedback is providing too much negative feedback. Some instructors feel they have not done their due diligence grading if they did not point out everything wrong in the student's paper. Additionally, the feedback can come across as judgmental of the person, rather than of the student's performance. Let's take a look at an example:

Sara,

This work is adequate, but most of your information here seemed to come straight from your textbook. You need help with your English. See an academic advisor.

Here the educator used unfocused, confusing comments. There is a dismissive tone and they have sent the message to the student that they should not ask the educator directly for support. Additionally, the educator was culturally insensitive in the way they communicated their feedback to the student about their comprehension of the English language. The example below offers another way to communicate the information in the example above.

Sara,

You have a good start here. You were able to discuss important points from this week's learning resources. To improve your work, start to work on synthesizing the ideas from your textbook with your own thoughts about this week's topic. It might be helpful to print out the rubric and keep it next to you as you develop your work. Also, I noticed that some of your sentence structure needed editing. I was able to point out one or two examples in your paper. I have posted some grammar and writing support resources in our online classroom. I have no doubt with focused efforts on writing and English comprehension your work will continue to improve.

Here the educator used the sandwich method of providing feedback and was able to provide the feedback in an educative manner. The student was told exactly how her work could improve, and what resources the student could use to work on improving their work. Additionally, the educator did not overwhelm Sara with feedback. She pointed out one or two places in Sara paper where she made the mistake, without fully editing her whole paper.

Educators can sometimes go overboard and provide too much feedback. Students will become overwhelmed and shut down when this happens. If a student really missed the mark, consider meeting with them one-on-one. Also, think about ways you can provide feedback in broad categories. The feedback to Lisa demonstrates how to list out major areas of concern that she needs to work on, without providing too much detail.

> Lisa,
>
> I noticed that you made several good arguments in your paper. There are a couple of areas that are in need of improvement:
>
> - Developing a strong argument means using literature from authors that support and criticize your position. You listed several authors who support your idea. For future assignments, remember to include authors that also challenge your position.
> - To make a good argument, you need a solid writing structure. You do not want to have just a list of good ideas. You will need some transition sentences to help your reader not only understand what you reading but why you're making the argument.
> - I want to recommend proofreading your paper a couple of times over. There are some good software applications that I have listed in the classroom that can help you with spelling and grammar concerns.
> - Finally, I want to recommend printing out the assignment rubric. Before you submit your assignment, grade yourself using the rubric for the assignment.
> - You make some really good points in your papers. If you use this feedback to guide the development of your future work, I am confident your work will improve.

Here the educator was able to provide Lisa with broad areas of content that she will need to pay attention to improve her work while providing concrete steps to make the improvements to her work. This example demonstrates the use of providing narrative feedback.

Many educators are pressed for time and providing this level of feedback is not always possible. A well-developed rubric would also be able to communicate what is listed in narrative form in the example above. This may take more time for educators during course development but will save tremendous effort and time once the course begins.

Quiz

1. Assessment practices in higher education:

    a. are used to evaluate student performance and provide guidance to faculty on course and program effectiveness
    b. have moved to being input-driven rather than outcome driven
    c. have remained relatively stable across the past three decades
    d. reflect a bottom-up shift driven by individual faculty members

2. The type of assessment that provides student feedback and is intended to be incorporated in future performance is:

    a. evaluation feedback
    b. formative assessment
    c. summative assessment
    d. formative evaluation

3. Best practices in counselor education assessment include:

    a. informing students of the assessment process in orientation
    b. informing students of how they will be assessed in an on-going capacity
    c. sharing with students the evaluation measures that will be used for the assessment process
    d. all of the above

4. The ACA Code of Ethics reflects a counselor educator's responsibility to:

    a. provide detailed and lengthy feedback to students in the evaluation process
    b. use assessment practices as part of their larger gatekeeping responsibility
    c. evaluate student performance for the purposes of modifying their own teaching practices
    d. evaluate student knowledge and skills as the most significant indicators of fitness for the profession

5. Which of the following is not a necessary condition for increasing faculty "buy in" to the assessment process:

    a. requiring faculty to develop individual assessments for their courses
    b. providing necessary training on the assessment process

    c. engaging faculty in the development of assessment processes and practices

    d. regular communication on the purpose and needs of the assessment process

6. Which of the following does not provide students with the best opportunity to master the necessary knowledge, skills, and disposition necessary for the counseling profession:

    a. a variety of assessment opportunities throughout the program

    b. a strong reliance on summative evaluation

    c. a developmental approach where learning is scaffolded across time and experiences

    d. a mixture of learning experiences

7. Comprehensive exams are an example of what type of assessment:

    a. knowledge assessment

    b. skill-based assessment

    c. summative assessment

    d. both a and c

8. A mid-term evaluation of a student's on-site practicum performance could be an example of all of the following except:

    a. formative assessment

    b. dispositional assessment

    c. summative assessment

    d. skill assessment

9. One benefit of a holistic rubric is:

    a. it allows for independent analysis of various criteria

    b. it allows for an evaluation of global performance in a given area

    c. it provides the opportunity to score criteria separately

    d. both a and c

10. Which is *not* a noted benefit of rubrics:

    a. they provide clarity for students on what is expected of performance in a given area

    b. they provide opportunities for students to be active agents in their own learning process

    c. they allow for enhanced norm referencing

    d. they allow for greater objectivity in the evaluation process

11. If a faculty member is developing a skill-based rubric and is establishing the specific criteria she wants assessed in the rubric, she is developing her:

    a. evaluation criteria
    b. performance categories
    c. performance descriptors
    d. scoring metric

12. Rubrics that demonstrate high intra-rater reliability result in:

    a. consistent scoring for different students by the same faculty member
    b. consistent scoring for the same student by the same faculty member
    c. consistent scoring for the same student by different faculty members
    d. both a and b

13. The term associated with the extent to which scores on a rubric actually predict future performance is:

    a. content validity
    b. criterion validity
    c. outcome validity
    d. construct validity

14. Which of the following is not a noted benefit of using assessments in the gatekeeping process:

    a. they allow for comparison of performance relative to an established benchmark
    b. they provide objective feedback that can be used to support the remediation process
    c. they guarantee student fitness for the profession
    d. they model the importance of assessment practices in the larger counseling profession

15. Which of the following is the best approach to minimizing student anxiety and resistance to the assessment process:

    a. providing ungraded peer review of assignments
    b. reducing the number of assessments used to evaluate students
    c. providing open and on-going communication about assessment practices
    d. using only summative evaluations

9 The Role of Gatekeeping in Counselor Education

Counselor educators serve as gatekeepers to the profession. It is their ethical obligation to ensure counseling students develop and deliver competent counseling to clients. When counselor educators notice students struggling or deficient in a skill, knowledge, or disposition, it is their gatekeeping obligation to the public to ensure students remediate the deficiency. This chapter will offer experiential and applied exercises to deepen understanding of issues related to teaching and being a gatekeeper within the educator role for a program, university, and profession.

- Remediation plan case studies with reflection questions

- Case examples for gatekeeping

- Quiz

Remediation Plan Case Studies with Reflection Questions

Ljubica Spiro

The following are two remediation case studies with sample plans, guidelines for assessing completion, and informed consent documents to use with students when developing a plan. Following these comprehensive examples are reflection questions to help you devise your own remediation plan.

Case Study 1

Student Issue

Melanie is a second term counseling student. She is currently enrolled in Dr. Jones's online Counseling Theories course. She became very concerned with her grades and her instructor's feedback half way through the term. Melanie believes the instructor is being unfair and insensitive to her personal circumstances. She decided to email the Program Chair, Dr. Smith, with her concerns.

> Dr. Smith,
>
> I need your help. Dr. Jones is treating me unfairly. I think she doesn't like me because she keeps taking off points for what she says are "late submissions". She doesn't seem to understand that I work fulltime and am a single mother. The only time I can complete my work is on the weekends. So, I have to submit my papers a couple hours past the deadline. I informed her about my situation the first week of class, and she said she would work with me. Well that hasn't been the case. I've tried to schedule a time to meet with her, but she is only available until 7 PM EST. Well I'm not available until 8 PM. She refuses to make any concessions. I thought this program was set up to meet my needs as a working adult. I WOULD LIKE TO CHANGE SECTIONS ASAP!!!
>
> Sincerely,
>
> Melanie

Melanie communicated with her instructor the first week of class to let Dr. Jones know she had not received her text and may be late completing her first assignment. She also shared that she was having some work-related issues that may interfere with her ability to submit her first two assignments on time. Dr. Jones has attempted to schedule meetings with Melanie to discuss her grades and inability to stay on track, but Melanie has missed both of the meetings because of work.

Areas of Concern

- Melanie is struggling with professional maturity. She reached out to the Program Chair before she ever spoke with her instructor. Melanie is presenting as defensive and inflexible.
- Melanie blamed others or external factors for her own academic problems, professional deficits, and/or interpersonal difficulties.
- Melanie has time management issues and may need to re-evaluate her school and work schedule.
- Melanie used technology inappropriately and disrespectfully.

Remediation Plan with Measurable Outcomes

FRAMEWORK FOR REMEDIATION PLAN

ACA Code of Ethics 2014, Section C, Professional Responsibility. Counselors aspire to open and accurate communication in dealing with the public and other professionals. They practice in a nondiscriminatory manner within the boundaries of professional and personal competence and have a responsibility to abide by the ACA Code of Ethics. Counselors actively participate in local, state, and national associations that foster the development and improvement of counseling. Counselors advocate to promote change at the individual, group, institutional, and societal levels that improve the quality of life for individuals and groups and remove potential barriers to the provision or access of appropriate services being offered. Counselors have a responsibility to the public to engage in counseling practices that are based on rigorous research methodologies. In addition, counselors engage in self-care activities to maintain and promote their emotional, physical, mental, and spiritual well-being to best meet their professional responsibilities.

ACA Code of Ethics 2014, Section H, Distance, Counseling, Technology, and Social Media Counselors understand that the profession of counseling may no longer be limited to in-person, face-to-face interactions. Counselors actively attempt to understand the evolving nature of the profession with regard to distance counseling, technology, and social media and how such resources may be used to better serve their clients. Counselors strive to become knowledgeable about these resources. Counselors understand the additional concerns related to the use of distance counseling, technology, and social media and make every attempt to protect confidentiality and meet any legal and ethical requirements for the use of such resources.

Action Steps

- Student will be redirected to contact the instructor and share concerns via email.
- Student will make appropriate accommodations to meet with the instructor during office hours.
- Student will be provided an opportunity to have another faculty on the call for additional guidance.
- Student will review class syllabus and review the deadlines for assignments and consequences for late submissions.
- Student will review Student Code of Conduct.

Plan

Student will meet with her assigned faculty mentor to address areas of concern. Melanie will be placed on a remediation plan for the next 4 weeks. The student will begin working on the plan after first scheduled meeting with faculty mentor, and will have all elements of the plan completed by the end of the term. Failure to complete all tasks will result in further remediation.

The student will be able to submit each of these assignments 2 times. Faculty mentor will provide feedback and student will be expected to implement the feedback.

I. Time management activity

   a. Student will create a weekly calendar to include all activities and identified times for studying and completing homework. Student will identify at least 12 hours of weekly study time.
   b. Student will submit the schedule to faculty mentor by the close of business Thursday for review.
   c. Student will adhere to schedule and make modifications as necessary.

II. Netiquette

   a. Student will review the **ACA Code of Ethics 2014, Section C, Professional Responsibility and ACA Code of Ethics 2014, Section H, Distance, Counseling, Technology, and Social Media.**
   b. Student will review University Student Code of Conduct.
   c. The student will compose an email to the instructor asking for assistance and/or clarification. The student will identify specific needs, and provide the instructor days and times she can meet. Student will make appropriate accommodations so she can meet within the specified office hours.

III. Self-Care Plan

   a. Student create a self-care plan using the Maintenance Self Care Worksheet as a Guide.

Case Study 2

Jay is a second-year counseling student who is currently enrolled in a group counseling class. Jay's GPA is a 3.6. He's a motivated and eager student. His professors have described him as hardworking, dedicated, and at times over zealous. Jay has a history of challenging grades and accepting feedback. He's a pleasant student but seems to have difficulty managing his anxiety. When he doesn't receive a response to his emails about his grade within 24 hours he begins to send multiple follow up emails. His professors have brought this to attention, but he seems to have a hard time exercising patience. This term Jay's behavior in class has become increasingly disruptive to his peers. Jay continues to monopolize classroom discussions. His feedback to peers is direct and at times abrasive. Jay's faculty and one peer have provided him with feedback about how he is being perceived, but Jay dismissed it. He felt he was being misunderstood. His professor became concerned and referred him to the Student Development Committee for additional support and guidance.

This is Jay's second career. A few years back he decided that he wanted to pursue his dream and become a counselor. So, he left corporate work and became a fulltime student.

Table 9.1 Development Plan Rubric		
Time Management Activity	Student will create a weekly calendar to include all activities and identified times for studying and completing homework. Student will identify at least 12 hours of weekly study time. (10pts)	
	Student will submit the schedule to faculty mentor by the close of business Thursday for review. (10pts)	
	Student will adhere to schedule and make modifications as necessary.	20 points
Netiquette	Student will review the **ACA Code of Ethics 2014, Section C, Professional Responsibility and ACA Code of Ethics 2014, Section H, Distance, Counseling, Technology, and Social Media.**	
	Student will review University Student Code of Conduct.	
	The student will compose an email to the instructor asking for assistance and/or clarification. The student will identify specific needs, and provide the instructor days and times she can meet. Student will make appropriate accommodations so she can meet within the specified office hours.	
	Student will write a 2-page reflection paper addressing the importance of following the ACA Code of Ethics, University Code of Conduct, and online netiquette when sending professional communications to faculty and supervisors. (40 pts)	40 points
Self-Care Plan	Student will create a self-care plan using the Maintenance Self-Care Worksheet	30 points
Attend all Scheduled Meetings	Student will attend all scheduled meetings with mentor and schedule a call with faculty to address concerns.	10 points

Failure to complete all tasks may result in further remediation.

Table 9.2 Development Plan Rubric 2		
Johari Window	Separate directions have been provided.	40 points
Professional conduct	Student will review the **ACA Code of Ethics 2014, Section C, Professional Responsibility and ACA Code of Ethics 2014 and Section D, Relationships with Others.** Student will review University Student Code of Conduct. Student will review university grade appeal process and adhere to the policy. Student will write a 2-page reflection paper addressing the importance of following the ACA Code of Ethics, University Code of Conduct, and grade appeal process.	20 points
Self-Care Plan	Student will create a self-care plan using the Maintenance Self-Care Worksheet. Student will focus on managing anxiety.	30 points
Attend all Scheduled Meetings	Student will attend all scheduled meetings with mentor.	10 points

Failure to complete all tasks may result in further remediation.

Areas of Concern

- Student is struggling with interpersonal boundaries.
- Student lacks self-awareness. His behaviors are impacting his peers' education.
- Student is unable to consistently control his emotions.
- Student has difficulty accepting feedback.

Remediation Plan with Measurable Outcomes

FRAMEWORK FOR REMEDIATION PLAN
ACA Code of Ethics 2014, Section C, Professional Responsibility. Counselors aspire to open and accurate communication in dealing with the public and other professionals. They practice in a nondiscriminatory manner within the boundaries of professional and personal competence and have a responsibility to abide by the ACA Code of Ethics. Counselors actively participate in local, state, and national associations that foster the development and improvement of counseling. Counselors advocate to promote change at the individual, group, institutional, and societal levels that improve the quality of life for individuals and groups and remove potential barriers to the provision or access of appropriate services being offered. Counselors have a responsibility to the public to engage in counseling practices that are based on rigorous research methodologies. In addition, counselors engage in self-care activities to maintain and promote their emotional, physical, mental, and spiritual well-being to best meet their professional responsibilities.

   ACA Code of Ethics 2014, Section D, Relationships with Others. Professional counselors recognize that the quality of their interactions. with colleagues can influence the quality of services provided to clients. They work to become knowledgeable about colleagues within and outside the field of counseling. Counselors develop positive working relationships and systems of communication with colleagues to enhance services to clients.

Actions Steps

- Student will meet with faculty mentor to address the areas of concern.
- Student will review all rubrics for class assignments.
- Student will limit participation in class discussions while he works on development plan.
- Student will wait 48 hours before following up with instructors.
- Student will review Student Code of Conduct.

Plan

Student will meet with his assigned faculty mentor to address areas of concern. Jay will be placed on a remediation plan for the next 4 weeks. The student will begin working on the plan after first scheduled meeting with faculty mentor, and will have all elements of the plan completed by the end of the term. Failure to complete all tasks will result in further remediation.

The student will be able to submit each of these assignments 2 times. Faculty mentor will provide feedback and student will be expected to implement the feedback in order to successfully complete the development plan.

I. Johari Window Exercise and Paper
    a. Student will write a 3–5page paper in APA format

II. Professional conduct

    a. Student will review all rubrics
    b. Student will review all guidelines for assignments
    c. Student will review grade appeal process before he challenges and future grades
    d. Student will write a 2 page reflection paper about what he learned about the grade appeal process and adhering to the code of ethics.

III. Create a self-care plan

IV. Attend all scheduled meetings

Reflection Questions

- How would you have handled the first instance of student comportment concerns? Would you have done anything differently in either case?
- As the Program Chair in the case of Melanie, what would you have done if you had received this email? What else could Dr. Jones have done once learning of Melanie's contact with the Chair?
- Are there additional comportment issues you would want to address?
- What do you think of both action steps and plans? What would you add? Change?
- In terms of the assessment of the plans (rubrics), would you add or change them in any way? How and why?

Case Examples for Gatekeeping

Laura R. Haddock

Consider the following case examples. After reading the case, answer the subsequent questions.

Case 1—Deena

Deena is a student in your Research Methods and Program Evaluation Course. She actively participated during week 1 and 2 of the course but then did not submit any assignments for week 3. Upon reaching out to her via email, you learn that Deena suffers from depression and has had a really tough week. You offer her a time extension to complete her work and she contracts with you to have the outstanding assignment in within 7 days. Deena does not submit the assignment and essentially drops out of the course only to reappear in week 7 and request an opportunity to catch up on all outstanding work and finish the term.

- What are the gatekeeping issues of concern for this case?
- Should Deena be allowed to continue in the course?
- If so, what are the implications of that decision?
- If not, what is the rationale for that choice?
- Are there ethical or legal concerns at play in this case?
- Is remediation or professional development appropriate?

Case 2—Edward

Edward is a student in your Introduction to Mental Health Counseling Course. He reports that he is transferring from another university, though you have no information about why he has changed programs. Edward emails you after he receives feedback on his week 1 assignment and questions your grading and demands a higher score. After agreeing to review the feedback, you determine that the score is appropriate and in accordance with the rubric. Edward becomes enraged with your refusal to award additional points and sends an email to the department chair complaining that you are an incompetent instructor.

- What are the gatekeeping issues of concern for this case?
- Who should be responsible for responding to Edward?

- What are next steps for you as the professor?
- Are there ethical or legal concerns at play in this case?
- Is remediation or professional development appropriate?

Case 3—Cynthia

Cynthia is a second year student in the school counseling program who has a history of strong academic work and a very professional disposition. She has excellent relationships with her peers and has been consistently responsible and responsive to faculty. You overhear her peers laughing that Cynthia has alcoholic beverages in her insulated cup during virtually every night class and that she has "snowed everyone".

- What are the gatekeeping issues of concern for this case?
- Should you confront Cynthia about the information you have overheard?
- If so, what are the implications of that decision?
- If not, what is the rationale for that choice?
- Are there ethical or legal concerns at play in this case?
- Is remediation or professional development appropriate?

Case 4—Otto

Otto is a third year doctoral student who recently finished his practicum hours. His final paperwork has been submitted and approved and he is scheduled to begin internship hours next term. Today, you receive an email from a source claiming to be Otto's ex-wife. She claims that she is also a counseling professional and that she was Otto's supervisor of record for his practicum placement. She tells you that she did actually provide Otto with supervision every week of his practicum, but that she feels guilty because she knows it was "against the rules".

- What are the gatekeeping issues of concern for this case?
- How should you proceed after receiving the email?
- Should Otto be allowed to count his practicum hours of supervision?
- Are there ethical or legal concerns at play in this case?
- Is remediation or professional development appropriate?

Quiz

1. Which of the following is NOT a 2015 CACREP classification for determining counseling competence?

   a. Skills
   b. Past experience
   c. Dispositions
   d. Knowledge

2. A skill deficiency is defined as:

   a. The normal expected challenges of learning a new counseling skill
   b. When a student appears incapable of developing a new counseling skill
   c. Both a and b
   d. Neither a nor b

3. There is a strong relationship between undergraduate GPA and GRE scores and dispositional factors necessary to become a competent counselor.

   a. True
   b. False

4. According to Bernard and Goodyear (2014), which type of evaluation elicits more discomfort in the supervisory process?

   a. Summative
   b. Oral
   c. Dispositional
   d. Formative

5. Counselor educators should remember the following recommendations when implementing a remediation plan:

   a. Provide prospective and current students with written documentation of performance standards
   b. Apply competencies and assessments consistently across all students in the program
   c. Develop remediation plans that are concrete, well-defined, and linked to program standards
   d. All of the above

6. When is the best time for identifying and addressing student deficits?

   a. At the end of the program
   b. During fieldwork
   c. As early in the program as possible
   d. At the time of candidacy

7. Which of the following is NOT a student level recommendation for dealing with students who demonstrate programs with professional competency:

   a. Putting the student on probation
   b. Increasing supervision
   c. Repeating coursework
   d. Ignoring the issue

8. Students should be kept informed at every stage of the remediation process.

   a. True
   b. False

9. According to Veilleux et al. (2012), what percentage of problematic students are identified by program faculty?

   a. Slightly more than 25%
   b. Slightly more than 50%
   c. Slightly more than 75%
   d. 100%

10. What exam measures student knowledge of the 8 core areas of professional counseling and is recommended for gatekeeping?

    a. NCE
    b. GRE
    c. CPCE
    d. ACS

11. "Gate slippage" refers to:

    a. A flawed admissions screening process in counselor education programs
    b. An expectation that others will fulfil the gatekeeping function
    c. Consulting with colleagues regarding the gatekeeping function
    d. Pressure from institutions to increase gatekeeping mechanisms

12. Why is the gatekeeping function so important?

    a. It is an ethical responsibility of counselor educators

    b. It helps prevent harm to future clients

    c. It ensures the well-being of other students in the counselor education program

    d. All of the above

13. Conversations related to counseling and multicultural competence should be avoided in discussions with problematic trainees.

    a. True

    b. False

14. Which is the best strategy for dealing with resistant students?

    a. Collaborate with the student in developing a remediation plan

    b. Spend limited time discussing deficits

    c. Avoid discussing strengths and successes

    d. Using combative confrontation

15. The gatekeeping function begins at pre-admission and continues until termination (e.g., degree completion or program dismissal).

    a. True

    b. False

References

Bernard, J. M., & Goodyear, R. K. (2014). *Fundamentals of clinical supervision* (5th ed.). Upper Saddle River, NJ: Merrill.

Veilleux, J. C., January, A. M., VanderVeen, J. W., Reddy, L. F., & Klonoff, E. A. (2012). Differentiating amongst characteristics associated with problems of professional competence: Perceptions of graduate student peers. *Training and Education in Professional Psychology*, 6, 113–121. doi:10.1037/a0028337.

10 Teaching Across Settings

Learning and teaching has transformed in the past decades in respect to delivery setting and medium. No longer is a face-to-face learning environment the only means by which counseling students seek education. Online teaching and learning has become more popular and convenient for students. This chapter will provide information and instruction for how to use technology in face-to-face classrooms, virtual classrooms, and hybrid class constellations.

- A guide to technological tools to be used to supplement the classroom

- Guide to facilitating active online discussion forums

- Quiz

A Guide to Technological Tools to be Used to Supplement the Classroom

Abby E. Dougherty

Below are a variety of technology tools you can use to enhance student learning and instruction. This is not an exhaustive list, as new tools are created continually. However, these tools are some that have been used consistently in counselor educators

Zotero
https://www.zotero.org/
Zotero is a free application that helps you organize your research. You can manage your articles, format citations, and will sync with multiple devices.

FlashBack Express
https://www.flashbackrecorder.com/express/
This application allows the user to screen record their desktop or webcam. Unlike many free screen recording applications, FlashBack Express has no time limit on the length of the recording and does not leave watermarks on your videos.

Join.me
https://www.join.me/
Join me is a free screen sharing and online meeting application. This is a wonderful application when you facilitate by sharing your desktop with your students.

Kahoot
https://kahoot.com/welcomeback/
Kahoot is a game-based application that allows educators to design quizzes that can be taken during class time using cell phone and laptops to answer questions in real time. Educators can design their own quizzes or choose to use many pre-developed quizzes from the applications library.

Prezi
https://prezi.com/
Prezi is a visual storytelling software application that offers an alternative to the traditional powerpoint presentation.

Rubistar
http://rubistar.4teachers.org/index.php
RubiStar is a free application that helps educators develop rubrics. There is also a searchable library of rubrics that user can edit and use for their own.

Google Classroom
https://classroom.google.com/
Google classroom offers educators the ability to develop online classrooms, assignments, and resources. This is a wonderful resource for flipped and online learning classrooms.

Grammarly
https://www.grammarly.com/
Grammarly is easy to use editing and grammar checking application. Grammarly can be used with applications like Microsoft Word, but it can also be used in within a variety of learning platforms. Students who are posting text directly into Blackboard can still check their writing for grammar errors before hitting the submit button.

Turnitin
http://turnitin.com/
This application allows both students and educators to review assignments for plagiarism.

Attendance Manager & Tracker
https://itunes.apple.com/us/app/attendance-manager-tracker/id896023706?mt=8
Educators can use this application to track attendance in classes. This application can be used on multiple devices and save and track attendance for hundreds of classes.

Freemind
https://www.mindmup.com/
Freemind is a free online mind mapping. A mind map is an easy way to brainstorm thoughts organically, yet still provides order and structure to your thoughts.

Evernote
https://evernote.com/
This application allows you to share and store notes from multiple devices. This free app is popular with academics in higher education.

Educreations
https://www.educreations.com/
Educreations is a simple to use whiteboard application. This software application has an easy to use software interface where you can draw, develop movies, and collaborate easily with students or colleagues.

Explain Everything
https://explaineverything.com/
Is an interactive whiteboard that can be screen-casted to students. Like Educreations, you can draw, develop movies, and collaborate easily with students or colleagues. While educreation offers simplicity with its interface, explain everything allows for depth and detail with their video editing tools. Educators can edit their videos easily using this application.

Dropbox
https://www.dropbox.com/
Dropbox offers easy to use cloud storage. Users can upload up to 20 gigabits of data for free with each account. One of the nice aspects of dropboxes is the application and sync with multiple devices, making it easy to access data from a laptop or Smartphone.

Slack
https://www.Slack.com
Slack is an easy to use application for teamwork. Slack provides an easy to use interface to chat with your team, share documents, and Slack integrates with popularly used social media applications.

PlayPostIt
www.playposit.com/
PlayPostIt allows teachers to create lessons and video assignments easily. Additionally, the application has real-time embedded assessments for educators to choose from.

Guide to Facilitating Active Online Discussion Forums

Laura R. Haddock

Discussion forums are a common element of hybrid, blended, and online classrooms. Learners have the opportunity to interact with peers and share experiences and meaningful online online collaborations can also improve knowledge retention and social learning skills. For instructors, facilitating active engagement in discussion forums can be a daunting task. Depending on the dynamics of the class make up, students can be non-responsive, monopolize topics, make inappropriate self-disclosure, or even demonstrate a lack of cyber civility. The following strategies may help engage students, promote critical thought, and keep distractions at a minimum are a key to facilitating meaningful online discussions.

Have A Conflict Resolution Plan in Place

Cyber civility is a necessary component of successful engagement in discussion forums. However, as the instructor, if you encounter conflict among or between students (or with you) it is important to have a plan in place for how to deal with it. Your role as the faculty member may require you to intervene and it is important to always stress the importance of mutual respect. You can also use conflict as a teachable moment to emphasize the importance of cultural competence, respect for differing perspectives, and the ethical responsibility of not imposing personal values or beliefs onto others.

Define Expectations

While course guidelines typically outline the minimum requirements for participation, communicating clearly about what you are looking for from students is a smart move. You must be clear about what learners can expect from you and what you expect from them. Specify how often they should post and what their posts should entail. You may even write a list of tips and guidelines and offer students to maximize potential for success.

Be an Active Participant in the Discussion

In some instances, meaningful online discussions run fairly autonomously, and learners take control of moving the discussion forward. However, your presence in the discussion is also important. Posting responses to student posts, offering additional resources, and prompts that encourage online learners to reflect or connect two or more participants within the discussion are good strategies for having a clear presence. Invite students to share feedback and voice their concerns. The goal is to motivate learners to invest in the process and want to participate.

Create A "Talking Point" Schedule

Whether you are developing the discussion or teaching a curated course, create a schedule for your own engagement that features all the topics you want to cover and when. Include all materials, links, and prompts or questions that accompany each talking point. You should also emphasize how each discussion topic relates to the learning objectives and goals for the course.

Quiz

1. Which of the following are strengths of face-to-face learning environments?

   a. Instructors are able to integrate technology creatively within their classes to enhance and deepen the overall learning experience
   b. Students are likely to feel a connection to faculty and fellow scholars on a seemingly more personal level
   c. Face-to-Face learning allows for subjective evaluation
   d. All of the above

2. All of the following contribute to the notion that hybrid classrooms may represent the best of both worlds in terms of learning outcomes for graduate counseling students except:

   a. The use of technology tools in hybrid classrooms covers more diverse learning styles
   b. Due to the increase in technology use in recent years, all students can incorporate technology tools in the classroom easily
   c. Greater flexibility in pace and scheduling
   d. Students have in person access to faculty and technological tools for self-directed, experiential, and active learning

3. Challenges of online education include:

    a. Inadequate instructor training may lead to feelings of discomfort related to technology use when teaching in online environments
    b. Time constraints may be a deterrent
    c. Students may perceive faculty as lacking in guidance and support contributing to feelings of isolation and decrease retention rates
    d. All of the above

4. All of the following contribute to the notion that hybrid classrooms may represent the best of both worlds in terms of learning outcomes for graduate counseling students except:

    a. The use of technology tools in hybrid classrooms covers more diverse learning styles
    b. Due to the increase in technology use in recent years, all students can incorporate technology tools in the classroom easily
    c. Greater flexibility in pace and scheduling
    d. Students have in person access to faculty and technological tools for self-directed, experiential, and active learning

5. Which of the following contribute to positive student faculty relationships:

    a. Encouraging students to feel they can have access to online instructors at all times via e-mail
    b. Engaging in clinical relationships with current students
    c. Creation of a trusting environment that enhances student comfort in peer-to-peer and student-faculty interactions
    d. All of the above

6. Student-faculty relationships are multi-dimensional. Counselor educators serve students in multiple roles, therefore:

    a. Instructors must attend to multicultural awareness and the power differential between students and faculty
    b. Maintaining balanced boundaries that support effective communication, consistent reflection of the benefits of student-faculty relationships, and explicit assessment strategies are imperative
    c. Instructors must engage in clear communication from the beginning of the relationship through the duration of the student's graduate program
    d. All of the above

7. When communicating with students, faculty must demonstrate all of the following except:

   a. Clear, concise, and respectful communication across educational platforms
   b. Effective communication of expectations from the beginning of the class
   c. Respect and support emotional reactions in the classroom
   d. Professional and civil tone in written student-faculty exchanges

8. Which of the following is counter to providing effective feedback:

   a. That which is simple and offers a quantitative evaluation
   b. That which offers a qualitative and quantitative evaluation
   c. That which utilizes various tools and encourages creative and critical thinking
   d. That which is immediate, specific, and balanced

9. There is an ever growing number of technology options for the classroom, therefore counselor educators need to consider many factors when choosing to incorporate technological resources in their classroom, including:

   a. Student learning style
   b. The American Counseling Association Code of Ethics guidelines on technology use
   c. Compliance with HIPAA and HITECH
   d. Instructor skill level
   e. All of the above

10. The authors of the Unified Theory of Acceptance and Use of Technology propose that there are:

   a. Very few persons of the millennial generation that are technologically illiterate
   b. Many factors that predict whether a person has the financial and technological resources to pursue online education
   c. Social and intrinsic values that influence a person's willingness to adopt technology use for different applications
   d. Too many technology resource options available for educational purposes and that researchers are working to combine and integrate systems to streamline technologies

11. Social media technologies include

    a. Facebook and Twitter
    b. Discussion forums
    c. Blogs
    d. Collaborative learning technology platforms
    e. All of the above
    f. a and c, only

12. Asynchronous technologies:

    a. Involve differentiated or separated communications.
    b. Do not require a timestamp for completed communication.
    c. Allow the technology user to communicate with others in a simultaneous, fluid environment.
    d. Include technologies such as video conferencing, telephone conferencing, and virtual worlds.
    e. All of the above.

13. Synchronous technologies:

    a. Is the connection of learning management systems with university registration and enrollment systems
    b. Include technologies such as virtual classrooms and video conferencing
    c. Do not require a timestamp for completed communications
    d. Represent forms of technology that emphasize the syncing of computer clocks across platforms

14. Virtual classrooms bring together multiple classrooms by audio-visual connection with cameras and video screens, particularly in special circumstances such as

    a. When a remote, inaccessible instructor provides a live demonstration of a science experiment
    b. When an instructor records a video of a classroom activity and uploads the video to a webpage accessible to other sections of the class
    c. When a classroom of students participates in a class activity on an occasion when the instructor cannot be present
    d. When asynchronous strategies would be a preferable approach to delivering class content

15. Virtual worlds are very involved video games such as World of Warcraft or Minecraft:

    a. But have very little application for classroom education purposes
    b. That may have classroom application where actual students play avatar students sitting in a classroom while listening to the instructor lecture
    c. That offer students an opportunity to control actions, expressions, and movements of avatars while communicating with other avatars and completing tasks of educational games
    d. That provide a great example of where classroom technology and gaming technology demonstrate competing purposes

11 The Role of Mentoring in Counselor Education

In addition to offering instruction to counseling students, counselor educators serve as mentors formally and informally. Developing a mentor identity is crucial to the success of counselor educators. To facilitate the development of that identity and role, this chapter provides exercises to deepen understanding of the process of mentoring students. It will include:

- Strategies for building mentoring relationships

- Case examples of effective and ineffective mentoring and guided questions

- Guided questions to explore personal and professional characteristics that may enhance and hinder effective mentoring relationships

- Quiz

Strategies for Building Mentoring Relationships

Marcella Rolle, Stephanie Fellenger, and Joy S. Whitman

In this section, we offer strategies for building mentoring relationships and offer suggestions from both the position of mentor and mentee. We recommend also using the chapter from the text to guide you as you develop your relationships with mentors and mentees. Both sides of the relationship require attention to fostering clear and consistent communication.

Suggestions for Mentors

- Assess what skills, knowledge, and personal and professional dispositions you possess that facilitate good mentoring and which ones you may need to enhance. Reflect on why you want to mentor new faculty or students and what kind of mentor you would like to be.
- Consider whether there are roles as a counselor educator for which you are more equipped to mentor. We are all not equally expert or experienced in all roles, and it is better to be up front with potential mentors about the roles in which you are most comfortable serving. Finding colleagues to whom you can refer your mentor and who can supplement where you are less skilled is great mentoring.
- When contacted by a potential mentee, discuss what they are looking for in a mentor and how they imagine you helping them. Ask them what their goals are for the mentoring relationship and what their time frame is for meeting those goals. Let them know whether you can mentor them toward those goals and whether their time frame will work for you. You can let them know if their goals are ones you can help them reach and in the time frame they expect.
- Get to know your potential mentee. Offer personal and professional information so that the relationship can be established on these levels. When offering personal information, decide what seems appropriate for them to know so that you are comfortable with your level of self-disclosure and the mentee has a better understanding of who you are as a person. Good mentoring relationships are above all ones that engender trust and respect, and mentees enjoy knowing who their mentor is beyond their professional accomplishments.

- Discuss identity differences and similarities between you. Mentees may be hesitant to discuss these differences. This is especially true when you mentor students whose social and personal identities are different from you. Effective modeling and mentoring requires open and clear communication as well as the ability to discuss important issues, especially ones where your differences might cause disagreement or may cause you to overlook something of importance. For example, a mentor who is Caucasian and lesbian mentoring a mentee who is heterosexual and African American will need to talk about their identities so that those social barriers and prejudices can be managed and myths dispelled.
- Respect your mentee's time and effort. They are busy either with their studies, dissertations, or new academic appointments. If you plan to meet regularly, attend those meetings or reschedule with their schedule in mind as well as yours. Ask for the same commitment from your mentees. In the end, your actions will speak volumes and engender the trust the mentoring relationship deserves.
- Finally, being asked to mentor someone new in the field is an honor. We suggest treating it as such and ensuring you enter into the mentoring relationship with the goal of helping your mentee grow. There is great reward in being on the journey with new professionals.

Suggestions for Mentees

- Assess your strengths and weaknesses, both personally and professionally. You want to connect with a mentor that accentuates your strengths and will work to improve your weaknesses. Through the assessment, you will gather an idea of what you are looking for in a mentor.
- Consider what is it that you want to achieve through the mentoring relationship. Are you looking to develop expertise in a particular content area? Gain writing and research experience? Are you seeking a mentor to help you navigate your growth as a future counselor educator across all roles or simply specific responsibilities to teaching, service, or scholarship? By reflecting on your goals, you can begin to identify appropriate mentors.
- Critically review the resumes and curriculum vitae of faculty that interest you. Make yourself knowledgeable about what potential mentors bring to the table. Essentially you are conducting an informal interview during which you can judge whether the nature of the mentor's work aligns with your goals and interests. Additionally, this helps you cut down on wasted time by trying to reach out to all faculty.

- Measure the strengths and weaknesses of each candidate against your strengths and weaknesses and look for comparable traits. You need not find a mentor that is a perfect match; rather you should look for someone who will help facilitate your growth. Consider whether the personality traits of you and your potential mentor will be a match. Even if similar research areas exist, a mentee looking for scheduled, regular interactions and a mentor who is more relaxed with communication (or vice versa) may both find themselves frustrated throughout the relationship.
- Once a final decision has been made, send out a formal request. Schedule a face to face meeting or video call with potential mentors. The feelings you experience in the presence of a potential mentor can make or break a mentoring relationship. You want to feel comfortable and respected. Often you can overlook these cues when meeting over the telephone.
- Introduce yourself, your interests, and your goals. Express to your potential mentors how his or her work in the field inspired you. Finally, use the results of your comparative analysis to present a well-defined argument for why a mentoring relationship between you and the counselor educator will enhance not only your life but the counseling community.
- Make sure to choose someone who is comfortable with the level of attention you are looking for. For example, were you hoping for monthly video calls or meetings to discuss your ideas? Did you want to eventually collaborate on a research project? Do you want your mentor to offer you tips for teaching and for you to perhaps observe them teach? Make potential mentors aware of these ideas so they can determine whether they are the best fit for you (most are happy to point you toward someone more in line with your goals, if needed).
- Set measurable objectives for your time together that are in line with your goals for the mentoring relationship. If you goal is to develop a research plan for a future study, hold yourself accountable with achievable targets that you complete between mentorship appointments. This might mean reading a certain number of articles between calls/video chats. It might mean creating a cover letter for an academic position or creating and refining your philosophy of teaching statement. Be transparent in your discussions of how the process is going. Your mentor is there to support you!
- Be mindful of how valuable your mentor's time is. Treat that shared time with great respect and enjoy the process!

Case Examples of Effective and Ineffective Mentoring and Guided Questions

Marcella Rolle

Case Example Effective Mentoring

Alaina is excited about her first official mentoring session with Dr. Jones. Over the past few months, Alaina studied the careers of Dr. Jones and a few other faculty members in Chicago University's master's graduate program. Recently, Alaina emailed Dr. Jones to ask her if she would be her mentor. Alaina chose Dr. Jones based on her interest in school counseling and work with children. Alaina hopes to complete an internship either with children in a mental health facility or school setting. Alaina was thrilled to find out that Dr. Jones has worked in both capacities and still serves as a chair at a local children's mental health clinic. Dr. Jones was impressed with the level of research Alaina put into obtaining an appropriate mentor and responded by saying so and agreeing to serve as her mentor. They both decided on a date, time, and location that would be convenient. Dr. Jones advised Alaina that they would have only 30 minutes for the meeting.

In preparation for the meeting, Alaina sent Dr. Jones a list of topics she would like to cover, giving Dr. Jones time to prepare and respond efficiently, given they only have 30 minutes to converse. When Alaina arrives, she notices how enthusiastic Dr. Jones appeared concerning her goals for the meeting and her future. This excitement ignited confidence in Alaina about her plans. Alaina reminded Dr. Jones of the topics she wanted to discuss, only to realize Dr. Jones had reviewed the email and prepared feedback for Alaina concerning each goal. Together they developed first steps for each goal Alaina wished to accomplish during her first semester. Alaina left the meeting feeling appreciated by her mentor and motivated to begin.

- What strategies did Alaina use to prepare for her initial contact with Dr. Jones that led to a successful outcome? How did Alaina express to Dr. Jones the value of her time and experience? What additional efforts could Alaina have taken to maximize the time and connection?
- Why did Dr. Jones' preparation for and interest in Alaina's goals ignite such confidence in Alaina?
- What are some responses you are looking for from a mentor that may enhance your confidence in your choices and goals for the future?

- What are some examples of goals you would address in your first meeting with your mentor?

Case Example Ineffective Mentoring

Students in the master's graduate counseling program at Chicago University are assigned faculty mentors at the start of their enrollment. Although students are not required to meet with their mentors regularly, they are encouraged to do so to assist with program responsibilities and professional development. Jessica is a first-year student at Chicago University and has no plans for professional development beyond earning her counseling degree. Jessica decides to schedule a meeting with her assigned mentor, Dr. Jones. Jessica plans to take all of Dr. Jones' advice and form her goals based on this information.

Dr. Jones is a former school counselor who encourages Jessica to get connected to local school systems and afterschool programs to gain a better understanding about working with children.

Additionally, Dr. Jones suggests that Jessica attend a few American School Counselor Association (ASCA) meetings with her. As the mentoring meeting continues, Jessica realizes she lacks an interest in working with children. Furthermore, she recognizes that Dr. Jones' experiences do not align with her future. However, Jessica feels stuck and does not speak up. At the end of the meeting, Jessica has agreed to attend an ASCA meeting and email the school counselor at the school where Dr. Jones once worked.

- What is one key strategy Jessica could have utilized to enhance the interaction in the meeting? Explain how this strategy would have improved the outcome.
- If you were Jessica, how might you have communicated with Dr. Jones when you realized her plans did not reflect your goals?
- What might Dr. Jones have done to invite input from Jessica? How else might she have started the mentoring relationship?

Guided Questions to Explore Personal and Professional Characteristics That May Enhance and Hinder Effective Mentoring Relationships

Sheila N. Russell

- Consider a mentor that you have had in the past that you think was a good mentor. What characteristics did they have that stood out to you? What made them a good mentor? What did they do to help you grow professionally and personally?
- Consider a mentor that you have had in the past that you think was not a helpful mentor. What characteristics did they have that stood out to you? What did you need from them that you did not receive? How did your experiences with this mentor impact you professionally and personally?
- What personal characteristics do you have that might enhance and hinder a mentoring relationship? Which of those characteristics do you need to develop so that they are less of a burden on a mentoring relationship? How might you ago about developing these personal characteristics?
- What professional characteristics do you have that might enhance a mentoring relationship? Which characteristics do you have that might hinder a relationship? How might you develop these characteristics so that they have less of a negative impact on a mentoring relationship?

Quiz

1. A conventional definition of mentoring has focused on peer-to-peer relationships.

   a. True
   b. False

2. Three aspects of the mentoring experience have emerged in the literature as key outcomes of effective mentoring EXCEPT:

   a. Clear vocational and personal guidance
   b. Socialization into the professional community
   c. Enhanced physical health
   d. Improved learning

3. Mentoring can be particularly helpful for women and faculty of color who are frequently marginalized in higher education.

   a. True
   b. False

4. When mentors serve as coaches, they can:

   a. Provide opportunities for collaboration
   b. Establish clear boundaries for teaching loads
   c. Take responsibility for mentees' travel to conferences
   d. Serve as the eyes of the administration and report misconduct

5. When mentees encounter problems or experience critical incidents, effective mentors see their responsibilities as:

   a. Avoiding blame
   b. Determining what the consequences should be for the mentee's error in judgment
   c. Initiating damage control and protecting the mentee
   d. Taking full responsibility for the mentee's culpability

6. Which is not a strategy for successful and effective mentoring?

   a. Nominating a student for an award
   b. Discussing a successful tenure portfolio with
   c. Considering privilege
   d. Favor elitism

7. What issue continues to persist as barriers to effective mentoring?

   a. Prioritizing elitism
   b. Disengagement from the mentoring process
   c. Mismatched goals between mentor and mentee
   d. All of the above

8. Successful mentoring can result in a systemic impact that provides enhanced outcomes for job satisfaction.

   a. True
   b. False

9. Faculty of color and women are not at risk of experiencing the glass ceiling in higher education and academia.

   a. True
   b. False

10. Mentoring carries a significant contribution to counselor education, but not necessarily to leadership development.

    a. True
    b. False

11. Quality mentoring experiences offer:

    a. Career advancement
    b. Theoretical understanding of a cultural theory
    c. Department politics
    d. Less independence in faculty development

12. How can a mentoring counselor educator assist with early career professionals and doctoral students advancement in opportunities?

    a. Communicating the need to act independently
    b. Providing a letter of recommendation or nomination
    c. Providing a syllabus without any guidance
    d. Communicating only about institutional guidelines

13. Collaborative opportunities include participation in a Chi Sigma Iota event and activities directly related to social justice.

    a. True
    b. False

14. When considering mentoring, which is not a part of the socialization process for doctoral students in counselor education?

    a. Identifying norms in professional organizations
    b. Helping doctoral students achieve a sense of community
    c. Assisting doctoral students with engaging collaborative scholarship properly
    d. All of the above are part of the socialization process

15. When recognizing a mentee's worth, which component is essential as a strategy?

    a. Offering membership information
    b. Selecting another student as a model of expertise and knowledge
    c. Highlighting a mentee's capability in a high-profile role
    d. All of the above

12 You Have Learned to Be a Teacher, What Is Next?

This last chapter offers you an opportunity to use the material from the book and the preceding chapters in this supplement to present yourself as counselor educators in academia. In this chapter, you will have an opportunity to explore a variety of activities and to review templates that will prepare you for the job search. We suggest using the templates and example questions as a starting point for putting together your professional dossier. What we offer are beginning points, and we encourage you to use the resources from the text to explore many other templates and examples. There is no one way to craft your CV nor your cover letter, so seek out mentors and other professionals who can offer examples of their professional documents. It will include:

- How to write a CV (template)

- How to write a cover letter when applying for a faculty position (example)

- How to search for faculty positions

- How to prepare for an interview (sample questions)

- Strategies when seeking promotion and tenure

How to Write a CV (Template)

Joy S. Whitman

We offer you a template to help you create your CV. You may have additional sections that are specific to your experiences, and we encourage you to include all that accurately represent your professional life.

CV TEMPLATE

Name
Professional Status or Position
Affiliation
Affiliation Address
Phone Number
Email Address
Website

EDUCATION

Year   University, City, State
                Doctoral Degree and Discipline

Year   University, City, State
                Master's Degree and Discipline

Year   University, City, State
                Undergraduate Degree and Discipline

PROFESSIONAL CREDENTIALS

Date   License

. . .

ACADEMIC EXPERIENCE

Date (start with   Position
most current and   Program and University
list all sequentially)
Description of roles and responsibilities.

. . .

PROFESSIONAL CLINICAL EXPERIENCE

Date   Kind of experience (for example, private practice)
                City, State

. . .

continued

TEACHING and COURSE DEVELOPMENT
Teaching

Affiliation (University name and program), Dates
List of courses number and names

. . .

Course Development

Affiliation (University name and program), Dates
List of courses number and names

. . .

AWARDS and NOMINATIONS

Award name, Affiliation, Year.

. . .

PUBLICATIONS and PRESENTATIONS

Publications—Peer Reviewed Journal Articles
References should be in APA format starting with most current.

Publications—Edited Books
References should be in APA format starting with most current.

Publications—Book Chapters
References should be in APA format starting with most current.

Publications—Nonrefereed
References should be in APA format starting with most current.

Conference Presentations—Peer-Reviewed
References should be in APA format starting with most current.

Conference Presentations—Invited
References should be in APA format starting with most current.

. . .

WORKSHOPS/PRESENTATIONS

References should be in APA format starting with most current.

. . .

GRANTS

References should be in APA format starting with most current.

. . .

MANUSCRIPT REVIEWER

References should be in APA format starting with most current.

. . .

SERVICE

Professional Association and National Leadership

Date   Name of affiliation and position

. . .

Academic Service—University (years)

Department level service
Membership position: Year of service
College level service
Membership position: Year of service
University level service
Membership position: Year of service

. . .

Community Service
Affiliation: Year; Member status

National Professional Membership
Affiliation (for example, American Counseling Association (ACA)

. . .

How to Write a Cover Letter When Applying for a Faculty Position (Example)

Joy S. Whitman

There are many ways to write a cover letter. Of most importance is to ensure you are qualified or have the majority of skills and experience stated in the advertisement for the position. However, if you have skills that are transferable to the ones outlined in the ad, speak to those skills and how they can meet the needs of the position.

The best cover letters are tailored to each part of the ad for the position. I suggest taking each stated requirement, skill, knowledge, and expectation and addressing it specifically. Let the search committee or whomever is reviewing your application know you read the ad, are familiar with the requirements of the position and with their department/college/university, and how your experiences can meet the stated needs of the position. Your CV will serve to supplement your application, and the cover letter lets the reviewer know who you are and what you can bring to the position more specifically.

What follows is a modified example you can use on which to pattern your own letter. It is a letter I crafted from a recent search, and though it is long, most are a page or two depending on your experiences. Again, there are ample examples for you to explore, and asking a mentor or other professional to review theirs is also recommended. You must develop your own style and let your personality come through in the cover letter.

COVER LETTER EXAMPLE

Name
Address
Phone number
Email address

Date
XXX Program
Address

Dear Dr. XX and Search Committee Members:

I am writing to submit my application for the Clinical Assistant Professor/Online Instructor position in the Clinical Mental Health Counseling Program at XXX University. Accompanying this letter of application is my curriculum vitae and my statement of teaching/supervision/clinical practice.

I have a strong interest in this position at XXX University where I would be a part of an online community of learners and faculty and an institution that actively connects to students nationally. Presently, I am Core Faculty in the XXX Program at XXX University where I teach in the doctoral program. I am looking for a position that will be primarily teaching and that will allow me to further develop my online teaching skills. To provide you with more detailed information about my qualifications and what I can bring your program and department, I will highlight my work in higher education and in counseling.

As I stated, I am presently Core Faculty in the XXX program at XXX University. I have been in this position for two years, and during this time I have taught courses on counseling theories, professional and ethical identity, foundations to the profession, and teaching in counselor education. I am primarily now teaching the course on teaching, and doing so has honed my skill and focused my career goals on best practices for the preparation of counseling students.

continued

As a result of my teaching this course, a colleague and I redesigned the outdated course curriculum. I have been teaching the new curriculum for the course for the past year, and it is more developmental and rigorous in design. I additionally chair many doctoral student committees as well as serve as content and methodology expert for others. It continues to be an honor to train our future counselor educators, and the position has permitted me to develop online teaching skills and strategies. XXX University has an extensive online training program for its faculty, and I have learned quite a bit about various forms of online content delivery. I regularly create videos to connect to students, interact with them on Blackboard during our discussions, and am available to them via email consistently. I am committed to online teaching and learning and have experienced first-hand how effective it can be.

Prior to my position at XXX University, I taught master's level counseling courses, and during that time, I taught a variety of courses as listed in my cv. Additionally, I developed new courses, such as counseling lesbian and gay clients, brief counseling, trauma and recovery, and supervision. I directed students' theses as their advisor and chair of their committee. Over the years, I integrated technology (such as Powerpoint and online videos) into my instruction. In 2009, I successfully completed a training offered by XXX University for faculty interested in teaching online courses. It was a three-week face-to-face and online workshop, introducing faculty to various online tools. After the training, I worked intensively with a staff member trained in online instructional design to transform one of my courses, Introduction to the Counseling Profession, into a hybrid class. I taught this course for many years as well as another course I transformed into a hybrid course (Counseling Theories) and integrated various mechanisms of information delivery. These included VoiceThread, podcasts, and Screenflow, and I successfully created my own podcasts, videos, and VoiceThreads. XXX University migrated from Blackboard to Desire to Learn (D2L), and I used D2L in all of my courses. Students commented on the usefulness of online discussions, the videos integrated, and the podcasts I either created or integrated from online sources. My goal was to address various learning styles and to reinforce learning by using multiple modalities of instruction.

I also want to highlight my experience in teaching a course in Mexico. During the winter intersession at XXX University in 2007, I took a group of students to Merida, Mexico, as part of a study abroad course focused on multicultural counseling. The impetus for this course arose from an initiative in the College of Education to address the needs of the growing number of individuals emigrating from Mexico. Students in the course enrolled in an intensive Spanish language class in Merida and engaged in service learning opportunities in Chicago after they returned. I am interested in issues of culture and social justice, and I am aware that one of the courses listed of interest for the position is multicultural counseling.

I have extensive leadership experience at university and professional levels. While at XXXUniversity, I served as the Chair of the department for two years, and prior to that, I was the Associate Chair. Throughout most of my tenure at XXX, I served as the Program Director of the XXX Program. While serving as Director, I also maintained a full teaching load and engaged in the other responsibilities of a contributing faculty member. In this capacity and during my first year at XXX, I realigned the curriculum in all three of the concentrations of the program to be consistent with state, national, and CACREP standards. My tenure at XXX University also allowed me to serve for a year as the coordinator of the counseling program. With that came the considerable task and opportunity to align the school counseling program with Indiana State school counseling and developmental standards. XXX University recently underwent a CACREP reaccreditation process, and the program coordinator and I were responsible for alignment of the doctoral program standards with CACREP standards. As a result of all of these experiences, I have gained knowledge and skill in leadership, and I am aware that the position in your department may include curriculum development. I will bring my years of experience at various universities to this

continued

position and feel ready to participate in the CACREP accredited
Clinical Mental Health Counseling Program.

I am also quite involved in the American Counseling Association
(ACA). I was the Governing Council Representative for the Association
for Lesbian, Gay, Bisexual, and Transgender Issues in Counseling
(ALGBTIC). I also served on the Executive Committee of ACA and was
reelected into that position. I was president and board member of
ALGBTIC and currently sit on the editorial board for the division's
journal. I also served on the editorial board for the journal for the
Association for Adult Development and Aging. I served on the Ethics
Committee of ACA and for many years, have been a conference
program reviewer for ACA. I find my commitment professionally with
ACA to be not only rewarding but also empowering, and over the
years I have encouraged and mentored students as they became
involved. I think it is important to be actively involved in the change
process, invested in one's professional organization, and to mentor
students into the profession. I would be happy to bring this experience
and my interest in student development to The Family Institute.

While at XXX University, I also served as the Clinical Director of the
master's counseling program. In this role, I coordinated students
enrolled in practicum and internship in schools, university settings, and
community counseling sites, and I organized, managed, and
coordinated the application of students applying for their clinical
placements for the next academic year. Additionally, I interfaced with
site supervisors and students when needed and university faculty
supervisors on an ongoing basis. I also created a training workshop for
faculty supervisors on supervision, and more specifically, on triadic
supervision. In the fall of each year we offered a clinical orientation to
students applying for practicum and internship, and I updated the
clinical handbook, organized the orientation, and facilitated the
delivery of this orientation. We also created a Blackboard and Desire
to Learn online site for students who were applying so that all
information and communication was centrally located. I served as one
of the faculty supervisors for a section in our community counseling

concentration, and I supervised and instructed a group of students in their practicum and internship. At XXX University, I was the internship supervisor for the students obtaining their degrees in mental health counseling. I understand the position at XXX will include practicum and internship courses, and I am capable of providing supervision and instruction to those students as well as working with site supervisors to ensure students are receiving quality experiences.

In terms of scholarship, I continue to successfully engage in scholarly activities such as national and international presentations, articles in refereed journals, and chapters in books. My focus of research has evolved to that of social justice for LGBTQQ clients and the preparation of counselors to ethically and professionally advocate for and provide counseling various LGBTQQ populations. I currently am in contract with The Haworth Press to co-edit a book that is a successor to a book my co-editor and I published in 2003. The title of the book is The Therapist's Notebook for Sexual and Gender Identity Diverse Clients: Homework, Handouts, and Activities for Use in Counseling, Training, and Psychotherapy. It is slated for publication in 2018.

My position at XXX sparked my interest in pedagogy from a scholarship vantage point. Before teaching at XXX, my interest in teaching as a subject was as a professor but not necessarily as an academic. As a result of my peaked interest related to the curriculum redesign of the course on teaching in counselor education, I am co-editing a book on teaching in counselor education. The title of the book is Preparing the educator in counselor education: A comprehensive guide to building knowledge and developing skills. The publication date is 2018, and my co-editor and I are in contact with Routledge Press. I am excited about the text that can serve counselor educators and doctoral students in counselor education programs.

I would like to highlight my work as a clinician as the position is one that requires experience in mental health counseling. I received a master's degree in community counseling in a CACREP accredited

continued

program and a doctorate in Counseling Psychology. I am a Licensed Clinical Professional Counselor in Illinois and a Licensed Professional Counselor in Missouri where I currently live. Through all of these opportunities, I have worked in varying clinical settings. These included counseling in a domestic abuse shelter, community mental health agencies, and university counseling centers. As a result of these experiences, I have become familiar with various ways of providing human services and the diverse needs of clients at different stages of life and with unique needs. My primary theoretical lens is psychodynamic with an emphasis on interpersonal theory and an integration of feminist principles. I will elaborate more in my teaching philosophy, clinical, and supervision statement. I maintained a private practice for over 16 years during which time I worked with individuals and couples. Since moving to Missouri, I have yet to establish a practice though I have offered consultation to those counseling lesbian couples.

I realize this letter of interest is quite long. I wanted to offer some context for my cv and how I can bring experience to the position. I am highly interested in this position and hope my candidacy for the position will receive serious consideration. Please feel free to contact me if I can provide any further materials to round out my application as you continue your search process. Thank you for your consideration.

Sincerely,
Signature
Name
Current Title/Position
University Affiliation

How to Search for Faculty Positions

Joy S. Whitman

There are many types of faculty positions, and finding the one that fits best for your personality, style of work, career goals, and personal life is important. However, no position will provide you with all you seek, and the possibility of starting with a position that offers opportunities for future advancement either there or at another university are things to consider. Below is a list of possible questions to ask yourself and to explore as you seek a faculty position.

Questions to Consider

- What professional goals do I have as an academic?
- What type of position will help me reach those goals?

  - Full time? Adjunct?
  - Online, face-to-face, or blended?
  - Tenure track?

- What are my skills and interests? At what university tier do I want to seek employment that will highlight and advanced my skills and interests?

  - Do I prefer to engage in research as my primary interest? Do I have the skills for a research position? Do I have the experience?
  - Do I prefer teaching as my primary interest? Do I have the skills for a teaching position? Do I have the experience?
  - Do I enjoy service to the profession and academy? Do I have leadership skills and experience?

- How am I qualified for the position?

- What experiences do I need to bolster my qualifications for the position I want and to fulfill my short and long-term goals? Will this position provide me with opportunities to bolster these qualifications?

- What university or college missions resonate with me? How will the mission fit with my career goals and, what supports do they have to develop my skills and interests?

- How mobile am I? Can I move and expand my search or do I need to stay local and tailor my search to those positions that are local? If local, what do I need to do to enhance my chances of a successful search?

How to Prepare for an Interview (Sample Questions)

Joy S. Whitman

Below are some typical questions asked during either initial phone interviews or on-campus interviews. It is important to do your homework and review each academic program, college, and university to where you are applying and tailor your responses accordingly. Some questions are generic, yet some are asked to explore what you know about the university and program specifically.

Included below these sample questions are ones you might want to generate when asked what questions you have. Having some readily available will also demonstrate you have done your homework.

Questions You May Be Asked

- What is it about our program that interested you? Why our program and university? Basically, what attracted you to this position?
- What experiences do you bring to our program that will contribute to its growth and to your teaching?
- Describe a challenging student experience and how you handled it.
- How would others describe you as a colleague? What do you look for in your colleagues?
- What is your research focus and how do you plan to develop it at our university?
- What is your teaching philosophy?
- How can you contribute to the growth of our program?
- What leadership qualities to you have, and what leadership opportunities would you like to pursue?
- How do you contribute to the profession, both in terms of scholarship and service?
- What do you consider the most critical issues in counselor education?
- What are your perceptions of professional identity issues in counseling and counselor education?
- How would you describe your theoretical orientation to counseling?
- What questions do you have for us?

Questions to Ask

- Can you tell me about your students? Where do they come from? How diverse are they?
- What are the expectations of faculty in terms of teaching load, scholarship, and service?
- What supports are there for faculty success? What resources are available to faculty to achieve promotion? And tenure if this applies.
- How are faculty mentored? Formally and informally?
- What opportunities are there for new faculty in terms of choice of classes to teach, service for the program/department/college/university, and research within the department and across the university?
- What are the program goals and how do those goals connect to the mission of the university?
- How is the counseling program, department, and college viewed at different levels of the academic community?
- What are the strengths and weaknesses of the program, department, college, and university?
- How are resources distributed among programs in the department, departments in the college, and colleges in the university?
- How many part-time or non-tenure-track faculty are employed in the department? Is the faculty unionized?
- What are the faculty members' teaching and research interests?
- How are decisions made among faculty members?
- What, if any, professional practice licenses do faculty members expect new appointees to have?
- How strong is the sense of community in the department and on campus? To what degree is there collegiality among faculty? What do you look for in your colleagues?

Strategies When Seeking Promotion and Tenure

Joy S. Whitman

Every university, college, department, and program has its own criteria for promotion and tenure. Most universities have information in their faculty handbook about the steps toward promotion and tenure and broad expectations for success. It is advisable to read through the handbook and consult with those in your program who have been successful.

It is smart to begin the process of understanding the promotion and tenure process at the interview stage. Find out what the history has been for those who have successfully been promoted and tenured in your college and department. This will help you know whether or not this position is right for you as well as begin to put together your professional dossier.

Once you know by what criteria you will be evaluated for promotion and tenure, begin to generate and collect the evidence to support your advancement. Here are some tips for each aspect of your dossier:

Teaching

- Normally includes:

  - Student evaluations
  - Reviews by faculty who have observed you teach (it is smart to ask senior faculty to observe you teach and to write a letter of that observation)
  - Awards for excellence in teaching
  - Sample syllabi
  - Course material you have developed
  - Explore what others in your department have included in their dossier.

Scholarship

- Either continue a research agenda you began as a doctoral student or new faculty or create a new one. Choose a path and direct your scholarship toward this.
- Examples of scholarship typically required:

  - Peer-reviewed articles and conference presentations
  - Books and book chapters
  - Grants
  - Non peer-reviewed articles and conference presentations,
  - Workshops (unless they are directed to your local community and not professionals and therefore better fit in the area of service), and
  - Other manuscripts

- Consult with senior faculty who can guide you in terms of what kind of scholarship is most valued in your department, college, and university.

Finally, there is a component of service expected from all faculty and that contributes to the advancement of your program, department, college, university, community, and profession. Here are some tips for service:

- It is wise to connect your service contributions to the focus of your scholarship as best you can. For example, if your scholarship has a focus of social justice, seek out opportunities at all levels of service that have a social justice focus or aspect.
- Use your scholarship and teaching knowledge across activities.
- Typical service experiences include:

  - Membership on committees at all levels of service noted above
  - Leadership within those committees
  - Membership or leadership at the local, state, and national levels of the counseling profession

- Look to more senior faculty for mentoring as they can help you make decisions about which service opportunities might be advisable to enhance your portfolio.

For each activity in which you engage as described above, ensure you have some evidence of having engaged in it and record of your contributions. This may include letters from other faculty who chair committees in which you are a member, letters of acceptance for manuscripts that are not yet published but are accepted, and student evaluations from each term. As you collect these pieces of evidence, begin to file them into appropriately designated folders. This will help you save time when it is time to present these documents formally and to keep you from scrambling to get the letter from a committee chair for the work you contributed to in that committee from five years ago. Remember, those who review your work will be combing through your portfolio in detail, and they will value accurate documentation that substantively paints the picture of the academic and counselor educator you purport to be. Let your professional dossier speak to your strengths and accomplishments, and let your accomplishments speak to your clear and followed journey as an academic.

Answer Key to Quizzes

Chapter 1 Quiz	
Question	Answer
1	C
2	C
3	A
4	B
5	C
6	B
7	A
8	D
9	D
10	A
11	A
12	B
13	B
14	A
15	B

Chapter 2 Quiz	
Question	Answer
1	E
2	A
3	B
4	E
5	C
6	E
7	D
8	A
9	B
10	E
11	A
12	D
13	A
14	B
15	B

Chapter 3 Quiz	
Question	Answer
1	A
2	C
3	B
4	A
5	B
6	D
7	B
8	C
9	B
10	D
11	A
12	C
13	C
14	B
15	D

Chapter 4 Quiz	
Question	Answer
1	C
2	A
3	D
4	B
5	D
6	D
7	B
8	D
9	B
10	D

Chapter 5 Quiz	
Question	Answer
1	C
2	D
3	C
4	A
5	C
6	D
7	B
8	A
9	B
10	D
11	A
12	C
13	D
14	B
15	C

Chapter 6 Quiz	
Question	Answer
1	A
2	B
3	C
4	C
5	A
6	A
7	B
8	C
9	C
10	A
11	B
12	C
13	B
14	C
15	B

Chapter 7 Quiz	
Question	Answer
1	F
2	C
3	C
4	F
5	C
6	D
7	C
8	A
9	E
10	E
11	B
12	D
13	A
14	B
15	A

Chapter 8 Quiz	
Question	Answer
1	A
2	B
3	D
4	B
5	A
6	B
7	D
8	C
9	B
10	C
11	A
12	D
13	B
14	C
15	C

Chapter 9 Quiz	
Question	Answer
1	B
2	B
3	B
4	A
5	D
6	C
7	D
8	A
9	B
10	C
11	B
12	D
13	B
14	A
15	A

Chapter 10 Quiz	
Question	Answer
1	D
2	B
3	D
4	B
5	C
6	D
7	C
8	A
9	E
10	C
11	E
12	A
13	B
14	A
15	C

Chapter 11 Quiz	
Question	Answer
1	B
2	C
3	A
4	A
5	C
6	D
7	D
8	A
9	B
10	B
11	A
12	B
13	A
14	D
15	C

Index